Copyright 2009 James W

Although this work has cop being reproduced or preacheu. ᴊᴏɪᴏmon said there is really nothing new under the sun and if the truth be known many of us communicators borrow from others. If this can be helpful to you in your ministry by all means use it. However if it is reproduced in a written form please give credit where credit is due, as I also have, with the many sources I've drawn from for this compilation.

If the book has been a blessing to you please let me know at;

James West Willows
PO Box 1896
Columbia Falls, MT. 59912

If you'd like to visit "HuckleberryLand" we are in Hungry Horse, Montana. We also have lovely cabins for rent on a nightly or weekly basis. Love and Faith Church is 4 miles east of Kalispell, MT. on Hwy. 35.
Email us at jwest1963@gmail.com
jaekyungwillows@gmail.com

To obtain additional copies of this book go to Amazon.com

Unless otherwise noted all scripture quotations are taken from the New International Version (N.I.V.) of the Bible. Copyright 1973,1978,1984 by International Bible Society.

I dedicate this book to everyone who is broke.

Table of Contents;

Each night the scurrying above the ceiling tile in our bedroom grows louder. Nightly ear plugs and pillows around my head are not enough to drown out the racket so I finally get up the nerve to make a ladder out of crates and push the ceiling tile up. Switch on the light in a dark room and your feelings will promptly react to what the light reveals - "Jaekyung, hand me the flashlight." The light and I peer into the attic. With a shiver I behold a scene from a horror flick; many sets of upside down eyes on large toothy bats which look like rats with wings. The Jamaicans informed me that these gross gargoyles are called "Rat Bats."

As poor missionaries to Jamaica this was our fourth rental home within a year's time. Our first lodging in the island was "The Ramble Great House" in the hills of St. Anne. They called it a *great house* because, as the slaveowner's mansion, it was much larger than any other house of it's era. The ornate mansion was more like a haunted house. Although, in it's prime, the Queen of England had bathed in our tile tub - the place was now in shambles. The first night was like sleeping in a zoo. The second night I trapped 5 mice and a rat in our bedroom. The third night I set up my 2 man tent inside the bedroom to keep critters out. When you are dirt poor you learn to get by. But there came a time when we said goodbye to the shamble in Ramble and made our way to greener pastures. We rented a lovely clean home overlooking the sea in Montego Bay. But within' a month or two it was clear we could afford it no longer so we moved into a motel, which was great till we birthed a screaming infant and were asked to leave. (The hospital fee for Jaekyung giving birth to Josiah in the Montego Bay Hospital was $5.00 U.S. Dollars. This included a three day stay in a room full of 20 other moaning mothers who had just given birth.)

The gargoyle apartment was our fourth rental. It had been occupied by drug dealers and had rat bats in the attic and demons in the living room. You may not believe me but I saw an ugly brown cloud move through our living room. The atmosphere seemed to breed arguments until we took spiritual authority over the home which then ushered in the peace of Jesus. We planted a church in a ghetto then returned from missionary service in Jamaica to make our home in Montana.

Upon returning we owned only a cheap Corolla, two pillows, and a few carpentry tools. But through applying the principles I'm about to share with you, we have increased in every possible way. In 1990 we began pioneering our place in life from a 10 by 52 1962 model trailer with tequila soaked carpet, and holes punched in the walls. Today we enjoy a new 3,250 sq. ft home on 10 wooded acres which are home to red tailed hawks and deer. We began a home business in our carport, because my wife was too pregnant to wait tables any longer, and God prospered the business till now we operate from a brand new 5,450 square foot showroom/factory on 360 feet of prime hiway frontage. We started a church with one person in a living room and now have a lovely sanctuary on 5 acres with a growing congregation of 30 people.

Montana ranks toward the bottom of the USA economically, People here often make negative comments about how "you can't eat the scenery." But the truths I'm about to share with you worked for us even in Montana. We prospered in challenging times and you can too.

Conventional affluence teachers tell us to "get all you can and can all you get" but the amazing part of how God increased us is that we increased by giving. We had the privilege of giving generously into God's kingdom projects. We watched our money take kids off the street and put them into a loving Christian boy's home. We saw beggars given a means to support themselves. We beheld churches in developing countries expand their outreach and have what they needed to go on. We had the joy of making a difference by giving generously, yet we saw what we gave come back to us on waves of God's blessing! This must be what Jesus calls **"life more abundantly"**!

The exciting aspect of this teaching is that I've outlined the practical steps that God led us to take which brought us from poverty to abundance. These steps will become a trail from where you presently are to the land of "life more abundantly." These principles I am about to share with you will change your world, if applied, but before we get started consider a word of caution;

3 Jn 2 , Beloved I pray that in all respects you may prosper and be in health even as your soul prospers. NAS

We as believers tend to carry baggage from Christianity's dark centuries of monastic life where it was considered more virtuous to go without this world's goods. Although this concept was borrowed from eastern religion and pagan monasteries, it subtly worked it's way into the fabric of Christian thought until monks took vows of poverty and many Christians considered poverty to be Christlike.

This thought system began to unravel when Puritans such as rich John Winthrop espoused the Protestant ethic that taught that **religious freedom and economic freedom were linked,** that enterprise was a virtue, and that financial success need not preclude spiritual salvation. (John Winthrop, "A Model of Christian Charity" 1630) Instead the Puritans were contemptuous of the old Roman Church's monastic belief that holiness required withdrawal from worldly economic concerns, and they preached that being industrious was a heavenly as well as a spiritual imperative. *For them making money was a way to glorify God.* As Cotton Mather put it in his famous sermon "A Christian and His Calling," it was important to attend to "some settled business, wherein a Christian should spend most of his time so that he may glorify God by doing good for others, and getting of good for himself." In their thinking, the Lord smiled on those who were diligent in their earthly calling. (Benjamin Franklin, An American Life, Walter Isaacson, page 10.) This is why our country was prosperous from the outset, they had a theological framework that supported being industrious in one's earthly, as well as one's heavenly calling.

Today, however, when the Bible's message of prosperity for the believer is preached it **still agitates** the spirit of religion which is deeply woven into Christian thought because of the years of monastic poverty vows. To confirm and elevate the controversy, some charlatan preachers have used the Bible's message of prosperity for unending personal extravagance and have tarnished God's word to the point that the unchurched openly stereotype preachers and mock "the prosperity message" with songs like, *"Lord won't you buy me a Mercedes Benz,* my friends all drive Porches I must make amends."

Because of this many sincere Christians have not embraced what the Bible says about prosperity and in this whole arena have been content to quote little proverbs like, **give me neither poverty nor riches but give me only my daily bread**...rather than embracing the entire word of God on this important subject. Because it agitates an inherited dark age bias towards poverty, many preachers avoid preaching God's word on prosperity even if they know it.

A believer and I were having a powwow about wether or not christians should have much money. He thought differently than I on prosperity so he was bringing out the typical arguments for Christians to not have much and I was sharing some of these truths with him. After going back and forth a little he summed up his position by reading the above cited cop out; "Lord, give me neither poverty nor riches, but give me only my daily bread. Otherwise I may have too much and disown you and say, "Who is the Lord?" Or I may become poor and steal, and so dishonor the name of my God." Proverbs 30:8-9

As I meditated on this text afterward I thought; the person who wrote that is a selfish sluggard, because he is only caring about his own needs, and his character is so unstable that if he

6

became needy he would steal rather than get a job. I further thought; surely a wise man did not write that proverb so I will check who did write it. I found that "Agur son of Jakeh" wrote it, and before he penned the text he confessed to Ithiel and Ucal; "I am the most ignorant of men; I do not have a man's understanding. **I have not learned wisdom**" Pr. 30:1-2 The man confessed he was an ignorant dummy at the outset so why make his conclusions your life standard? Some texts made it into the cannon of scripture not because they are correct but because God wants to give us an example of what ill-advised people think too. (Like Job's friends) A righteous person would never pen such words. A righteous man would say, "Lord help me make more money than I could ever personally use so that I can take kid's off the streets of thievery and prostitution and put them in Christian homes. So that I can fill up the coffers of those engaged in the cultural and spiritual civil war in America and the world. So I can rise up and make your church great, and so I can finance the preaching of the gospel to the ends of the earth."

Money is not evil nor is it the root of all evil but it is an amplifier. Money amplifies the ability of it's holder. The adulterer can go on a "sex cruise" instead of just taking a hooker to Motel 6. On the other hand the lover of God and of people can start an entire orphanage rather than just giving $10.00 per month to "World Vision." Money amplifies what is inside us. I am convinced **I can serve God better with money in my pocket than I can broke,** because I want to see his Kingdom come, and his will be done on earth, and this costs money.

I'd rather be a big blessing than a little blessing and I think deep down you would too because, if you are a believer, you are the seed of Abraham. His blood runs in your veins and his

7

DNA is in you somewhere trying to rise to the surface and impact your life's work.

God told Abraham he would be *BLESSED to BE a BLESSING* ! If we keep that mantra in mind it's easy to stay balanced as we embrace Bible prosperity.   If we do not it is equally easy to carve out only the portions of truth we like and use "the prosperity message" to prop up a grasping, indulgent lifestyle.

The human heart is by nature selfish and will produce selfishness; "me" and "mine" are some of the first words we utter when we begin speaking as toddlers.   On the other hand Christ's teachings are by nature unselfish and will produce unselfishness in us.   Therefore it is tricky to teach Bible prosperity accurately because if these truths fall on a selfish heart they can easily produce a justification for a self absorbed life. That's why I start my book saying, "use only as directed."   As we take this journey we must keep our focus on being a blessing, not on adorning our toilet with a gold plated seat.

Jesus said for a rich man to enter his kingdom ways he must first get through a very small door likened to the eye of a needle; God's door to the world of bible prosperity is GIVING. Jesus said " Give and it will be given unto you. A good measure, pressed down, shaken together and running over, will be poured into your lap." Luke 6:38.   The proverb says " He that refreshes others will himself be refreshed." Because the gate to Bible prosperity is giving, not getting, it is easier for a camel to go through the eye of a needle than it is for a rich man to enter the kingdom of God because the self absorbed will never enter through the gate of giving. They will refuse to tithe, refuse to give to the poor, refuse to let God have their two fish and five loaves, and in doing so, they will miss Jesus' invitation into the world of Bible prosperity. Tightwads may use the wisdom of proverbs to increase their net worth but will never really enter into the supernatural abundant life financially.

Jesus was offering the rich young ruler a chance to enter the door of the supernatural concerning Bible prosperity. Had he entered the door *by giving, like Jesus instructed,* Jesus would have multiplied back unto him one hundredfold in this lifetime, but instead of trusting in the LORD with all his heart he leaned unto his own understanding and walked away from the greatest financial offer of his life. And Jesus wept.

Kenneth Copeland is a man who gave his way out of overwhelming debt and learned to use the principle of giving to increase mightily on the earth. He learned that seeds produce after their own kind and sowed money to receive a harvest of money, cars to produce a harvest of cars, and airplanes to produce a harvest of airplanes. Many criticize him for flying a CITATION X, a premier executive jet, but I withhold my criticism because I happen to know he has given away at least 26 quality airplanes to missionaries, relief agencies, and other preachers. Jesus declared if we give it will be given unto us good measure, pressed down and running over therefore why should Christians gripe if the Lord's promise came true for Kenneth Copeland who reaped an airplane harvest?

Other preachers of prosperity I've watched have quoted the same scriptures Copeland cites but somehow underneath their thick stage makeup I detect a scam. Within a year or two I've seen them busted on 60 minutes for fraud or embezzlement. Because con men have tainted the true message many believ-

9

ers have thrown the baby of "the prosperity message" out with the bath-water.

The message of Bible prosperity is a powerful message and as with anything of power there is an element of danger if the power is not used appropriately. The use of this message all depends on the heart; is the recipient of the message a giver who desires to be blessed TO BE a blessing ? Or is the recipient a selfish person using God's word for personal profit ? I believe most who fall into error are not fiends or con men initially, but they begin to self delude and when they hit a tight spot they compromise their integrity.

Others have used the scriptures to do foolish or presumptuous things like buy things they could not afford in the name of "faith," only to have the items repossessed. But just because this message has been misused and mishandled will not hinder me from teaching you the truth of God's word that has enabled me to go from "rags to riches" in a state which ranks toward the economic bottom of the USA.

I shared Jesus' truths of giving and receiving to a needy teen from Jamaica named Devon. He had come from Flankers ghetto and was barely surviving caring for chickens. He obeyed God's word about giving and sowed a goodly portion of his meager income to the church we both attended. Before the week was over he found a large bill on the side of the road as he was walking home!

Gods' word will work in a ghetto, in a recession, in a depressed state, or for a habitual loser that is considered unlikely to succeed. God's word will work for you.

10

But this message of power must be handled with wisdom. Recognize your heart is deceitful and test yourself as you become a carrier of God's covenant prosperity to see if you have the money or if the money has you; Do you tithe ? Are you caring for the needy in practical ways ? Are you as excited to give as to get ? These are litmus tests that will let you do a check up from the neck up to see if you are serving God or serving money. Jesus said you can't serve them both.

Proverbs 1:32 says the prosperity of fools shall destroy them. (KJV) As you proceed with this message determine not to be a fool but to be a person who will use money wisely and to be a blessing.

This series is not meant to be a comprehensive guide to money management. There are many important subjects such as budget and debt reduction which are better covered in other works but this is a portion of God's revelation in the form of a Holy Spirit given acrostic expounding on 3 John 2.

3 Jn 2 , Beloved I pray that in all respects you may prosper and be in health even as your soul prospers.   NAS

The key to total life prosperity is a soul that is full of peace and connected to God.   Some people give everything they have for their business, and have made money, but they are selfish creeps without any true friends.   Others idolize health and fitness and have sculpted their body through weightlifting but have an empty soul.   One young guy at the gym I lifted at spent his free time lifting, drinking and partying.   His thought was, "if I make myself into a beast I won't have to care like a man."   He was healthy and his body looked great but his soul was suffering till he started to attend the church I pastor.   While we should be diligent in business and need to work out and keep fit we'll not experience the abundant life Jesus came to bring until our soul prospers through fellowship with God and His word.   That healthy soul then becomes the foundation off of which a materially successful and physically healthy life can be built.

Major league pitcher Daniel Naulty pitched three years for the Minnesota Twins before joining the New York Yankees for their championship run in 1999.   His deepest depression came on the heels of winning a World Series.   Drunk from the post game celebration and on the limo ride home with several teammates, he suddenly felt the weight of hopelessness and reached out to the only sober ears on board: " I asked the driver, 'Is this all there is to life ?"   The following day that question continued to haunt Naulty.   He says, "I thought the world series was going to be god, it was going to be salvation. But finding no comfort in the ensuing victory parades and parties, Naulty turned to God and the story of redemption he'd heard from Christian teammates. He began attending church and there felt God's conviction that it was really his addiction to performance enhancing drugs that had transformed him from a scrawny 86 mph. pitcher playing in the minor leagues to a 95 mph stud that had beaten others out for a roster spot and had just won a world series. He accepted Christ, went public with his steroid use and found peace in his soul. (WORLD Jan. 2008, "I'm deeply sorry".)

He had money, fame, strength of body, and health yet his soul was not at rest. Even after reaching the pinnacle of his sport... a world series championship, he plunged into a deep depression because he was empty,let down, unfulfilled. But when he came to know Christ HIS SOUL BEGAN TO PROSPER. Only then could he begin to prosper in all respects EVEN as his soul prospered.

So the prosperity God brings is not a band-aid for low self esteem or an attempt to gain significance. The prosperity of God flows out of a soul that is forgiven, a soul that is free, a soul that is satisfied, and a soul that is full because it is connected to God through Jesus and the Holy Spirit. Romans 5 says therefore being justified by faith we have peace. It doesn't say therefore being justified by faith we have money. Our prosperity begins with a soul that is healthy, connected to God and therefore has peace. David described it like this, 1. The Lord is my shepherd. 2. Therefore I shall not want. 3. He prepareth a table before me is such a way that MY CUP RUNNETH OVER. Bible prosperity is the overflowing cup of a healthy soul.

In the world of fitness core strength is central - abs, back, shoulders--the core of your body. If your core is strong it will be reflected in good posture and over-all health. When you are young you can get away with neglecting core strength but as you get older if you don't keep your core strong all kinds of posture, back, heart, and obesity issues surface which become major not minor problems. The recession our country is experiencing (2009) is an outgrowth of neglected core strength as a nation. The historical U.S. values of trusting and serving God, earning more than we spend, and holding to sound banking practices gave us great core strength as a nation. But when these core issues were neglected the current outgrowth of recession was inevitable. The answer to this is to begin to get our core - our soul - strong so we can prosper as our soul prospers. (Core strength revelation by Casey Treat)

This Bible starts and ends with the people of God walking in total life prosperity.

God's original man Adam and his wife Eve were
    healthy physically,
        sound mentally,
            and extremely well provided for.

Adam didn't own a silk suit, Eve didn't have a designer wardrobe, but no-one can argue the fact that they were extremely well provided for - They had it made in the shade, CEO's of Eden.com and loving it.

Then they did the unthinkable. They stepped outside of God's logical and loving limits through disobedience. They, as representatives of mankind, forfeited paradise and the total life prosperity God had provided but the good news is that Jesus came, as a representative for all mankind, to re-establish what they lost. Romans 5:17 says; By one man's offence (Adam) death reigned through that one man, HOW MUCH MORE! will those who received God's abundant provision of grace and the gift of righteousness REIGN IN LIFE through Jesus Christ!

I like these words HOW MUCH MORE. John 10:10 says Jesus came to bring us a life MORE ABUNDANTLY. One translation renders that as " a life that is better than you ever dreamed of." Adam forfeited total life prosperity but Jesus came to re-establish what he lost and the manner in which he did it was so awesome that anyone who tasted the new and improved abundant life would have to exclaim, "HOW

MUCH MORE?" The V.W. bug has become an icon but the original ones didn't quite get the bugs out. My sisters 1971 VW had a heater that barely worked and the creature comforts of a plastic outhouse. But when V.W. decided to re-introduce the beetle our friends who were doctors purchased a silver 2000 model with a cush leather interior, a sporty turbocharged engine, and a heater that actually worked!. I'm sure our friends who bought it didn't just say, Great we can buy a beetle again. They'd have to exclaim HOW MUCH MORE! of a beetle this is than ever before. Say it out loud, "HOW MUCH MORE!" **How much more** will those who receive God's abundant provision of grace and of the gift of righteousness REIGN in LIFE through Jesus Christ!

I like that term, **God's abundant provision of grace** , did Adam blow it, yes! Have you sinned, yes! Some of you were like me, you had a P.H.D. in sinning ! Nevertheless when you came to him, Jesus was the surgeon who injected God's abundant provision of grace into you to not only cure forever the sin problem but also give you a blood transfusion from the King of Kings that will enable you to now REIGN IN LIFE! Reign in LIFE, not reign in heaven, not reign in the sweet by and by, but reign right on earth in the rotten here and now !

Reign, that's a kingly term, reign in life. God's intention is that his reborn children reign in life like a king reigns over a kingdom. Not that life would reign over you, not barely makin' it in hopes that you might win the lottery someday. But reigning in this present life like a king reigns over a kingdom.

King David was a type of messiah was he not? A Man after God's own heart, slayer of the strongman, deliverer of God's people. Well what was the result of his ministry? The result

16

of his ministry was more gold and silver and peace than the world had ever known. The result was the reign of Solomon.

When the queen of Sheba heard of Solomon's fame; his wisdom and prosperity, she came to Jerusalem with a great train full of rare gems, gold, and spices. When she saw him reigning in life she concluded in verse 6 of I Kings chapter 10. "It was a true report that I heard in my own land, but I didn't believe the report till I came, but now that I've come I can see I wasn't told half the story for your wisdom and prosperity exceeds the fame of which I heard. Blessed be the Lord thy God which delighted in thee"

You see it's time that God's sons and daughters rise up and begin to reign in life. When the report of our prosperity reaches the ears of the kings and queens of this world they will just have to exclaim "Blessed be the Lord thy God which delighted in THEE!!"

True believers should not be surprised by double digit unemployment or by the dark reports coming from the evening news. God predicted in his word that gross darkness will cover the people but he still told the believer, rise and shine for your light has come. In other words God intends to put us on display to the world in a dark moment in history so that the kings and queens of this world will just have to exclaim "Blessed be the Lord thy God which delighted in THEE!!"

The religious traditions of man within the Christian church have talked God's people into living like a nun under a habit or a monk under a hood. They've talked us into believing that God delights when we are poor, struggling, and barely getting by - but this heathen queen had sense enough to realize that the tremendous prosperity that attended Solomon's reign was a sign of favor and of the fact that *God delighted in him.*

17

Psalm 35:27 "Let them shout for joy, and be glad, that favour my righteous cause: yea let them say continually, let the Lord be magnified, which hath pleasure in the prosperity of his servant." (KJV.) Religious tradition taught us that God is magnified and has pleasure in us struggling and doing without this world's goods, but the word of God declares that the Lord is magnified and takes pleasure in the prosperity of his servant.

The word translated prosperity in Psalm 35 is the Hebrew word Shalom. We think of "shalom" as a word that means peace. But Shalom means TOTAL COMPLETE WELL-NESS in every area of your life. You've heard this word Shalom used as a Jewish greeting: "Shalom my brother." What they are saying by that is PEACE To you and yours , may it be well with you,
> may your family be blessed,
> > may all of you be healthy,
> > > may there be plenty to eat upon your table,
> > > > and may all your endeavors succeed!

So the verse says God takes pleasure in the Shalom of his servant! GOD TAKES PLEASURE
> *in the Wholeness of his servant!*
> > *in the well being of his servant!*
> > > *in the health of his servant!*

Our salvation begins with peace but it doesn't end there. This abundant provision of Grace will produce wholeness in every area including you finances.
God is NOT saying I take pleasure when your   saved   but you're sick.
God is not saying I take pleasure when your healthy but you're broke.

18

God is not saying I take pleasure when you have money but you're full of fear.
No, in the verse God is saying I take PLEASURE when I see you;
*Prospering in your **spirit**,*
*Prospering in your **body**,*
*Prospering in your **marriage**,*
*Prospering in your **family**,*
Prospering in your bank account;
   driving your good car,
     living in a good house,
       giving generously into my KINGDOM,
        being delivered of your sins,
         being delivered of you debts,
          A ND increasing in the earth!

I'm tired of Christians representing God as if he takes pleasure in you eatin' hamburger helper without the hamburger in it.

I'm tired of Christians representing God as if he takes pleasure when they drive some old jalopy that they have to run behind and hop in then pop the clutch to even get it to start!

They can persecute me and call me a prosperity preacher all they want to, but while they're persecuting me, I'm gonna have wholeness-

     I'm gonna have peace-

I'm gonna drive to the bank and make a deposit, and lift up my hands and praise God all the way home because I found out that my broke days are over with forever. Because one of my father's names is EL SHADDAI which means the God who is MORE THAN ENOUGH! And EL SHADDAI delights in the prosperity of his servant!

19

Oh, I used to serve a god that kept me broke and proud of it. I used to serve a god who kept me siphoning gas to go places and sniffin' gas to get high.   But that god's name wasn't Jesus, that god was Satan and when Jesus kicked him out of my life that spirit of poverty had to go too.

El Shaddai is after wholeness, he's after total life prosperity and once you find that out,
then you won't PUT UP with the Devil constantly messin' with your finances.
Then you won't PUT UP with that debt that never goes away.
Then you won't PUT UP with talking like a victim because you live in Montana, or because there is a recession.
You won't PUT UP with religious traditions that keeps you in the darkness.
Because you will declare that God takes pleasure in the prosperity of his servant!
You will speak out the blessing of God over everything you touch,
and your angels will be quick to hearken to fulfill the words of your mouth !
    (Portion in italics is from Dr. Creflo Dollar's audio cassette, 20 Biblical Principles For Debt Release)

Did you ever stop and think why, before you were a christian, you always spoke out God D__n it !?   Satan knows there is power in your words so his influence on your darkened spirit inspired you to unknowingly curse your own life and bring YOUR LIFE into HIS AGENDA of poverty and a curse.   I used to speak that curse over my truck, my job, and other aspects of my life and it worked - my truck, my job, and my life didn't prosper.   But now that God's Spirit lives in me, and inspires my words, I've turned the power of my words around and I say GOD BLESS the work of my hands, GOD BLESS my business, GOD BLESS my children, GOD BLESS my cars. Just as the words of cursing used to produce results now my words of God's blessing produce results.

We must remember that God desires to bless us; The Lord remembers us and will bless us; He will bless the house of Israel, he will bless the house of Aaron, he will bless those who fear the Lord small and great alike. May the Lord make you increase, both you and your children. May you be blessed by the Lord, the Maker of heaven and earth. The highest heavens belong to the Lord but the earth he has given to man. *Psalm 115:12-15*

Since God's word declares that the MAKER of heaven and earth has placed a blessing upon me and a spirit of increase that MAKES me increase I must gladly begin lining up my words and my life with that blessing because it applies to me !

Most everyone who reads the Bible knows that God greatly blessed his servants in the Old Testament; Abraham was rich. Job was rich then he got twice as rich. Solomon was so rich that in his day silver was of little value because gold was so abundant. Joseph was sold into slavery but the blessing on him caused him to become the wealthy prime minister of Egypt by age 30. (Not bad for a slave.)

So there are many Old Testament examples of prosperity, and there are many Old Testament scriptures about prosperity be-ing the reward of the righteous, yet some think all of that ended when Jesus showed up. They say; "Ya but all that ended when Jesus showed up, Jesus was poor and he told us to deny ourself and become just as poor as he was."

I'd like to give a three-fold response to that statement:

1) Compared to what he had in heaven, Jesus did make a huge sacrifice in coming to the earth to become our saviour. But part of the reason he did it was so that the curse of poverty would be broken and each man and woman would live a blessed life; *For you know the grace of our Lord Jesus Christ, that though he was rich, yet for your sakes he became poor, so that you through his poverty might become rich.* 2 Corinthians 8:9

Some would reply, "that means spiritually rich, it's not talking about being financially rich!" One of the main rules of Bible interpretation is that you take scriptures in the context of the thought being presented by the author. If you examine the context of 2 Corinthians 8 it is in the context of Paul exhorting the believers concerning a needed financial offering, then Paul gives great promises of how God loves and will not forsake a cheerful giver and will bless their obedience to give by making all grace abound to them so that they under all circumstances and whatever the need will be self sufficient so that they will abound in their giving to "every good work." He tells them that God will increase the seed they have sown and multiply it back to them. The whole context is financial so when Paul says "that you through his poverty might become rich" he is not talking here about spiritual riches. (Though we know from other scriptures that this is included.)

We don't have to stay poor to glorify Jesus any more than we have to stay in our sins to glorify him. He became sin so we could become righteous and he became poor so that we might become rich. We should however follow his sacrificial life.

He gave up much to help others. In that same spirit we are to sacrifice our comfort, our money, and our goods in order to help others and advance his kingdom. But when we do, Jesus says the gifts we've given will be multiplied back to us even 100 fold. The material blessings Jaekyung and I enjoy today are because of the hundredfold return upon our sacrifices.

2) Though he was poor compared to what he had in heaven he was not poor and penniless on the earth.

A. Before he was even born 3 kings from the east came with a caravan of camels to present him with the 3 most valued substances in all the near east; gold, frankincense, and myrh. Kings from the east didn't hitch-hike with a few coins in a sock, they didn't travel 2,000 miles in a camel caravan just to present a future king with just a few coins like in the Christmas play. Their caravan and their presence was significant enough to get noticed by King Herod and to inspire him to slaughter thousands of Hebrew males out of fear of the King they were seeking. So before Jesus was ever born God made grand provision for his life.

B. *Joanna the wife of Cuza, MANAGER OF HEROD'S HOUSEHOLD, Suzanna and many others were contributing to Jesus' support from their private means.* Luke 8:3 Jesus wasn't broke ! Some rich ladies were contributing regularly to help support he and his team.

C. Jesus had enough money that he needed a treasurer.
Why would Jesus need a treasurer if he was broke? Judas was his treasurer, and even though Judas stole often from the purse, they still had enough to give generously to the poor and to purchase food and supply the needs of Jesus and his 12 full time staff members.

Why wasn't the perfume sold and the money given to the poor ? It was worth a year's wages. He (Judas) did not say this because he cared about the poor but because he was a thief; as keeper of the money bag, he used to help himself to what was put in it. John 12:5-6 When Judas was about to betray him Jesus told him to do it quickly. Those watching made this observation; *Since Judas had charge of the money, some thought Jesus was telling him to buy what was needed for the feast or to give something to the poor.* John 13:29

D. Jesus did change the emphasis of just prospering here on earth to doing everything we do to forward the eternal kingdom of God. The Old Covenant didn't talk much about life after death, but Jesus introduced a new perspective by saying that our life on earth is as a vapor compared to eternity. Therefore his view was that we should focus on building up the kingdom of God on earth and in heaven and that as we seek that kingdom first all our needs would be added unto us. As mentioned earlier this should help us keep our focus centered on his kingdom, but that kingdom needs funding to be successful.   As a missionary to many countries I've often organized teams to go with me to hold crusades and strengthen churches.   But many tell me, "I can't go with you brother James, no money." The number one reason many fail to be Christ's hands and feet is always finances.   So those who function as "kings" and bring provision into the church and missions projects are greatly needed. (In planting a new synagogue the team the Jews would send to a new city consisted of one rabbi and ten businessmen.)

It's very important for us as believers to realize this because Bible prosperity is not the same as the American Dream. The American Dream is to get all you can and can all you get, sacrifice family, marriage and friends if you have to, but get

24

ahead financially whatever the cost. Bible prosperity, on the other hand, is loving God, prioritizing your family, serving the gospel, being generous with his kingdom, then watching God multiply back to you every seed you have sown ! Even though Jesus switched the focus to an eternal kingdom he placed a high priority on doing well financially in the earth so that you could advance that eternal kingdom in the here and now and then HIS will would be done here on the earth, EVEN as it's already being done in heaven !

The kingdom of God is like a man going on a journey, who called his own slaves and entrusted his possessions to them. To one he gave $5,000.00, to another $2,000, and to another $1000.00, each according to his ability; and he went on his journey. Immediately the one who had received the $5,000.00 went and traded with the money and gained $5,000.00 more. In the same manner the one who had received the $2,000.00 gained $2,000.00 more. But he who had received the $1000.00 went away, dug a hole in the ground and hid his master's money.

Now after a long time the master of those slaves came and settled accounts with them. The one who had received the $5,000 came up and brought $5,000.00 more saying, "Master, you entrusted $5,000.00 to me see I have gained $5,000.00 more." His master said to him, "Well done, good and faithful slave. You were faithful with a few things, I will put you in charge of many things; enter into the joy of your master." Also the one who had received the $2,000.00 came up and said, "Master you entrusted $2,000.00 to me. See I have gained $2,000.00 more. His master said to him, "Well done good and faithful slave. You were faithful with a few things, I will put you in charge of many things; enter into the joy of your master."

And the one also who had received the $1,000.00 came up and said, Master, I knew you to be a hard man, reaping where you did not sow and gathering where you scattered no seed. And I was afraid, and went away and hid your talent in the ground. See, here is what belongs to you.

His master replied, you wicked lazy slave, you knew that I reap where I did not sow and gather where I scattered no seed. Then you ought to have put my money in the bank, and on my arrival I would have received my money back with interest. Therefore take the $1,000.00 away from him and give it to the one who has $10,000.00. For to everyone who has, more shall be given, and he will have an abundance; but from the one who does not have, even what he does have will be taken away.

Throw out the worthless slave into the outer darkness; in that place where there will be weeping and gnashing of teeth. (Matthew 25:14-30 N.A.S. with today's equivalent in terms of the dollar amounts inserted.) Verse 29 says the faithful slave will have **an abundance.** God is not against his servants having an abundance, on the contrary the Bible teaches that faithfulness will produce abundance.

Jesus said the kingdom of God was all about taking the money you'd been entrusted and making increase for the King and his kingdom. Some people constantly question what God's will for their life is yet this parable makes that question very clear. God's will is that you use the money, time, talents and abilities he's given you to produce increase for the King and his kingdom the church. So that his kingdom would come where? ON EARTH as it is in heaven. So here again we see the master delighted in those who excelled financially for the sake of his Kingdom.

Jesus taught in Luke 16:10 that If you have not been trustworthy in handling worldly wealth who will trust you with true riches (spiritual wealth) But when you are a good steward of finances God not only gives you more to steward over but he entrusts you with spiritual revelation and spiritual privilege in his Kingdom !

So we see that God's intent for man and woman in the beginning was abundance. We see that those who pleased him were abundantly blessed in the Old Covenant.We've dismissed some myths that Jesus our example was a penniless vagabond. We see that advancement in his kingdom has to do in part with how we use the money and resources he's given us to make increase for the church. Then the word of God concludes with God providing a city whose gates are precious stones and whose very pavement is translucent gold. **Prosperity from start to finish!**

You may be thinking, great that's what I need, but how do I ever obtain God's prosperity for my life. I'm glad you asked because what I have done here in this book is not only give you a revelation concerning God's desire to prosper you, but I've broke it down into manageable steps that you can take that will lead you into Bible prosperity. The teaching tool I'm using for this is an acrostic. An acrostic is where the ABC's of a subject are arranged according to the letters they correspond with. Proverbs 31 is an acrostic meant to teach the ABC's of how to find or how to become a wife of noble character. Psalm 119 details the love relationship between a believer and the word of God. Each section of the psalm begins with a letter of the Hebrew alphabet. In this acrostic I've taken each letter of the word prosper and attached to the letter a significant step on the journey toward Bible prosperity. Let's get started with the opening letter of the word; P is for plan.

27

People with many channels of TV love the remote because they can just recline on the sofa with their chips and easily control what they want to watch. One of my female kinfolk had been with a guy for over five years who had over 100 channels of Satellite TV. After being ignored as he reveled in his television she finally deduced that he loved TV more than her ! As she prepared to terminate the relationship she spitefully hid the remote then informed him that their 5 year long relationship was history and dramatically walked out of the house for the last time. In desperation her former sweetheart came running out of the house after her, but instead of saying, "baby come back" he exclaimed, "baby what did you do with my remote ?!"

That's a pathetic application of the remote, but as you view your life in view of God's desire to prosper you then you must realize that the remote is in your hand.
Your decision and the decision path you choose will dictate what you will be watching in your life in the months and years to come.

So take the time to plan,
          to chart a course of action,
             to design your life with a definite aim.
  They say if you fail to plan then you plan to fail but a failure to plan does not always mean failure but it does mean drift. If you fail to plan and define clearly stated objectives then you plan to be doing the same thing in five years as you are right now. If you don't set your rudder through having a clear plan you will just drift along with the current and will find

yourself in the same situation five years from now as you are right now. If you are 100 % satisfied with your life and believe you have peaked in every respect and you love everything you do on a day to day basis then fine. For the rest of us however we need a God given vision, a goal, and an objective for our life. Then we need to plan in detail how we will reach that objective.

A plan is " a method for accomplishing an objective" (Say it) Usually **a plan involves "a drawing or diagram showing the parts and details of a thing."** Many people have an objective but very few have a plan, which is a detailed , drawn up method for accomplishing that objective.

Wether for good or for evil there is power in a plan. At the tower of Babel in Genesis 11:6 God looked down and said, they've come together as one man with a common objective (vision/language) therefore I can tell that *"nothing they plan" will be impossible to them.* When you get a plan even the impossible becomes achievable. In their case God didn't like the self glorifying motivation for their plan so he came down to confuse the language. (Communication is so key for a group of people to achieve a plan, when their communication was scrambled their plan was aborted.) Had they planned something for God's glory or to benefit people God would have come down to help them. Not hinder them as God did at Babel. The point however is that there is power in a plan.

God has a plan, He's a "man with a plan." He has specific plans for your life, *For I know the plans I have for you declares the Lord, plans to prosper you and not to harm you, PLANS to give you a HOPE and a FUTURE. Jer. 29:11*
So according to this text God has plans for you, plans that will

result in a hopeful future. Plans to prosper you. So my friend if God has plans to prosper you, then you'd be smart to *tune in to God and get the plans* !

There are general plans revealed in the Bible which will work for anyone who will put them to work. Proverbs 21:3 says the plans of the diligent lead to profit as surely as haste leads to poverty. Diligent people with a plan are usually on the road to profit. Proverbs also states "He who gathers money little by little makes it grow." That means getting ahead financially isn't a leap it's a carefulness in the details that allows you to make progress. These proverbs will produce for believer or unbeliever alike.

Another general plan that works for every believer who will apply faith is 2 Cor. 9:6 *But this I say, He who sows sparingly shall reap also sparingly; and he who sows generously shall reap also generously.* This corresponds exactly with Jesus' teaching in Luke 6:38 *Give and it shall be given unto you; good measure, pressed down, shaken together, and running over shall men give into your bosom. For with the same measure that ye mete, withal it shall be measured to you again.* (K.J.V.) When you ask God to bless you, he will, but the measure he uses to bless you will be the same measure you used to dispense blessing to his church, to the needy, and to world missions. If you use a little spoon, single digit giving, he'll use a little spoon to measure out your blessing. If you use a big spoon, double digit giving, he'll use a big spoon to measure out your reward. If you use a shovel, triple digit giving, he'll shovel blessing your way. If you use a truck, giving in the thousands, your reward will come by the truck full. If you use a supertanker, giving in the millions, you won't say, "the camels are coming" anymore you will say, the supertanker is on it's way to my house ! For with the measure you use it will be measured to you again. (Don't think it's not working for you if it's not instant, God's return on your investment does not work instantly it works continuously.)

This principle will work for anyone who will put it to work, it's a revealed plan to prosper from God's word. However I believe God has tailor made plans to prosper you. Plans which you must tune in to receive. Plans which will open up to you as you obey his voice. Behold the incredible prosperity which came as a result of *just one* of God's specific plans revealed to his servant; God showed Joseph what would come upon Egypt during a crisis. Many times when the world is experiencing a recession/ depression/ famine it can be a time of opportunity for the wise. The plan, the means to accomplishing an objective, which God showed Joseph was to build grain silos and store up for the coming famine. In verse 39 the text says, the plan seemed good. (Gen. 41:22-40) What plan is God's Spirit whispering in your heart ? Does the plan seem good and bear witness to the wise ? Just one of God's specific plans revealed to his servant produced vast and incredible wealth. Proverbs 13:22 says the wealth of the sinner is laid up for the just. It was laid up for Joseph and Israel and through a God given plan can come into your hands also !

The Dominion mandate God gave Adam, his beloved son, has never been revoked. God never intended for the mafias and the cults to control the wealth of this planet. God intended for the body of Christ, for his beloved sons and daughters to control the finances. But he's had an incredibly difficult time finding a man or woman who would rise up out of small thinking, rise up out of the hassles of everyday life, rise up out of the oppression of the enemy, and begin to have a heart for the world, a heart for souls, and a heart for his kingdom.

31

In fact *the eyes of the Lord search to and fro throughout the whole earth to show himself strong in behalf of those whose heart is fully his.* 2 Chronicles 16:9

Once he finds such a person God has a plan, wether the plan is in commodities, huckleberries, or real estate God has a plan, the plan will seem good, and the plan will work even in the midst of economic downturn. Say "GOD HAS A PLAN to prosper me." Say "I'm going to seek and find that plan." *Ye shall seek me, and find me, when ye shall search for me with all your heart. And I will be found by you saith the Lord and I will turn your captivity.* Jer. 29:13-14 *Who then is the man that fears the Lord ? He will instruct him in the way chosen for him. He will spend his days in prosperity and his descendents will inherit the land.* The Lord confides in those who fear him. Psalm 25:12-15 (Don't think God is going to give you great revelation to prosper if you are not fearing him by obeying his already revealed will in the word such as tithing... giving 10% to your local church.)

RW Shambach tells two memorable stories of his partners in ministry. The one was a workin' man who chose to give generously and hilariously into RW's ministry. Shortly thereafter the guy bought a one ton pickup and as he was replacing the fuel pump or something he noticed a bundle taped to the steering column with black electrician's tape. After slicing it open he found it was a wad of large bills. Some old farmer probably thought his wife had discovered "under the mattress" so he went for "under the steering column" instead, only to have "stored it up" for the righteous.

A second partner felt like buying a hill in some Alaskan community. At that particular time there was a recession in Alaska and a heavy equipment dealer was asked how business was. He replied, I'd be faring badly if it weren't for the guy who bought that hill outside of town. He's discovered a gold vein there and has been purchasing plenty of heavy equipment ! God has a ways and means committee that would blow your mind. He has WAYS and MEANS of prospering you that you haven't even thought of !

In Job the word describes God as *"He who holds the Pliedes in the palm of his hand"* is the one we are dealing with. The Pliedes is a constellation and when I speak this series I show people what it looks like from the Hubble telescope just to expand their faith.

As a missionary who has travelled to 30 nations. I can testify that this works in every nation wether poor or rich.

I preached a large crusade in Abidjan, Ivory Coast. The leader of the church of 400 who sponsored me, Zacharie Adetola, an African of "poor" origin, went to the town commissioner and asked for a great piece of land to establish their ministry.

He was denied but as he was leaving the office the receptionist said, If I were commissioner I'd give you some land. Zacherie said to her "within several months you will be the commissioner and when you are give us the land" Sure enough the prophet's words came true and within months she was promoted and gave Zacharie's mission one hectare (square kilometer) of land in a prime suburb that was worth thousands of dollars. The day I visited the land with pastor Zach the workers had killed a big snake. The land had a little snake problem but for those willing to "go in and kill the giants" it was a real blessing. God's arm is not shortened so that he cannot save.

Fasting and prayer and tuning in to God's voice is key in the revealing of the plan. Kenneth E. Hagin tells this story; I knew a man down in Texas. He had never worn a pair of

33

shoes until he was 12 years old. He had only a fifth grade education. But way back when money was money, he was a millionaire.

Two different people, one from California and the other from Minnesota who had been frequent house guests in his home, told me that this man told each of them the same thing.

He said to them both, "In all these years and in all these investments (that's how he made his money), I have never lost a dime."

That beats my record. How about yours ?

"Everything I have ever invested in, has made money," he told each of them on different occasions. Then he told them how he did it. "I always do this. When someone comes along with an idea, wanting me to invest in something, my first reaction is mental. Now I know when Jesus said, "When you pray, enter into your closet," that He didn't necessarily mean you have to get into a closet to pray. I know he meant for us to shut things out. But I have a large closet in my bedroom where I go to pray. I pray about it. I wait long enough -- until I hear what my spirit says. Sometimes I wait three days. Now I don't mean that I stay in there 24 hours a day. I might come out and eat one meal. Usually I miss a few. I come out and sleep a little bit. But the majority of the time I am waiting, just by myself, until I know inside by an inward witness what I am to do.

"Sometimes my head says, 'Boy, you would be a fool to put your money in that. You'll lose your shirt.' But my heart says, 'Go ahead and invest in it.' So I do. And in all these years, I have never lost a dime.

"Then again, someone comes along with a deal and my head says, 'Boy you had better get in on that one.' But I don't pay any attention to my head. I get in that closet and wait. Sometimes all night long I wait. I'll pray and read my Bible, but a lot of the time I just wait. I just get quiet until I can hear what

my heart says. When my heart says, 'No, don't do it,' and my head says,
'Yes, you'd better get in on it,' I don't do it."

What had this man done? He had learned to follow the inward witness and God had guided him in his business, until in the late 1930's and the early 1940's he was already worth two million dollars. That doesn't sound big now, but it was big then.

Do you think God loved him more than He loves you? No, but this man took time to listen to God. *He took steps and means and measures to wait upon God.*
(Kenneth E. Hagin, How You Can Be Led by the Spirit of God 1986 Rhema Bible Church)

1. God has a plan   2. God reveals his plan.

Amos 3:7 God does nothing without revealing his plan to the prophets.

Respect the prophets and preachers God places in your life.

When the man of God stands up and says, I want you to give generously into God's work this morning. Don't think, *ya right he just wants my money!* That preacher encouraging you to give could be the door to your blessing. Remember the prophet who came to the widow woman. She was about to go broke and starve to death and he had the nerve to say, make a cake for me first. It was all she had but she honored the prophet with what she had then the cruse of oil never failed to flow and a canning and bottling company was birthed overnight.

I've come to respect the prophets God has placed in my life. People whose ministries have changed my life, Kenneth Copeland, Morris Cerullo, Creflo Dollar, Benny Hinn, Ed Allen, Casey Treat, Jerry Savelle, Mike Hayes, Ken Peters, Ron Smith, Hal Curtiss.

As I sow into these men's ministries I've watched their grace and anointing come into the church I pastor. God is doing something special at Love & Faith Fellowship. One time there was a terrible drought that produced the worst fire season Montana ever had but the only clear day in August was the day of our outdoor concert. Then it got smoky again for 3 weeks and the word came to us in Haggai to build God's house and not delay and because of delay drought had come. We started to build again and that week the heaven's opened and rains quenched all the fires! When I personally guaranteed the note for the five acres and the church facility I was prepared to sell my lovely home if need be to ensure we stayed afloat as an infant fellowship. I never had to sell it but four years later I sold my home and built a much nicer bigger home because of God's blessing. I took care of God's house so he took care of my house ! (Not through my pastor's salary because for years I received little to nothing.) I've watched this same spirit of increase come upon those who are faithful at church with their giving and their time. God doesn't need a successful businessman. God will take the LAST and make them the FIRST. God will take a nobody and exalt him/her to a place of great stewardship. (I Cor. 1:26-31)

Kenneth Hagan tells of a kid in a church he once pastored. She was a retarded girl named Ollie. She spent 7 years in the first grade and still couldn't sign her own name. Even at age 18 Ollie would crawl around under the pews and act like a two year old.

But Ollie's cotton pickin' mother loved God and was always faithful to tithe and at age 18 Ollie gave her heart to Jesus. God began to awaken Ollie's mind. A serviceman married Ollie and Ollie faithfully saved the checks he sent home every month. When he came home from the war they started a trucking business. Later Brother Hagan revisited that community and asked, whatever happened to Ollie and that bunch? His host said, do you see that extensive new housing development on the other side of town? That's Ollie's development, she's one of the most respected business ladies in town and still a pillar of the church. So my friends don't underestimate yourself. The God you serve is a great equalizer of intelligence. He'll take that which is not to confound that which is. (Kenneth E. Hagin, How You Can Be Led by the Spirit of God 1986 Rhema Bible Church, in that book he calls her a fictitious name, "Mary")

1 Chronicles 28:11-12 David gave Solomon the plans of various aspects of the temple which he said the spirit had put in his mind. The Spirit put the plans in his mind.
Say it, "Holy Spirit, put God's plans in my mind."
Are you getting excited about entering a place where the original Jew starts putting plans to prosper you into your mind ?

3. Establish the plan through counsel

In 2 Chronicles 30 Hezekiah made a plan to celebrate the passover and shared the plan with the officials. The plan seemed good and right to the king and to the whole assembly (v.4) so they moved on it. If an influential king feels it wise to get counsel before proceeding why do you move forward without good counsel ? Plans fail for lack of counsel but with many advisors they succeed. Pr. 15:22

As important as advisors are keep in mind that too much advice can also cloud your thinking. It appeared that king David had primarily two advisers. In the Catholic Bible there is a book called Ecclesiasticus. In that book it says; Get counsel yes, but never forget the counsel your own heart gives you is probably the best because no one cares as much about your situation as you do." So balance the counsel you hear from others with the counsel your own judgement is giving you. Good judgement is so key for any leader. A few really bad decisions can undermine your credibility.

4. Your enemy has a plan against you so you better have a plan to counter it

In Ezra 4:5 the people of God began to rebuild a temple for God but their enemies heard about it and set out to hinder them. *(vs4) Then the peoples around them set out to discourage the people of Judah and make them afraid to go on building .(vs5) They hired counselors to work against them and frustrate their plans during the entire reign of Cyrus king of Persia and down to the reign of Darius king of Persia.*
Later they basically brought a lawsuit against the people of God and the government compelled them by force to stop. Eventually the government changed and they were able to resume the work.

As I am ordained by them, I watched Pastor Casey Treat and congregation build probably the largest church sanctuary in the NorthWest. The city council kept hindering them saying "no way" so they went about praying for council members to be voted out or replaced. After several years they crossed that hurdle. Then at a critical stage in the building project Casey was diagnosed with hepatitis C and had to undergo chemotherapy. He didn't miss a service even though he felt awful.

During these delays and hindrances the price of material shot up and greatly increased expenses. But they outlasted the opposition and after about 10 years competed the massive complex for the glory of God.

During Nehemiah's project the Arab's got angry when the wall reached half it's height and *"they plotted together to come and fight against Jerusalem and stir up trouble against it. But we* (Nehemiah and company) *prayed to our God and posted a guard day and night to meet this threat."* Nehemiah 4:8-9

You see the devil has a plan for your destruction,
  he has a plan to keep you down,
    he has a plan to keep you contained,
     he will attempt to hinder you,
      and frustrate your plans,
because he can not afford for you to take money out of his enterprise and channel it into God's enterprise. The other big tourist business like mine in my town is owned by multi-millionaires who are putting casinos all over Montana.

So Satan has a counter plan, a strategy to keep you hemmed in. So what about you? What is your plan to break through his walls of containment? What is your plan to rise up and shake off poverty and debt?

Jesus came preaching the year of Jubilee; He came preaching freedom to the captives. Jesus came bringing a burden-removing, yoke-destroying anointing ! Debt and poverty is captivity, but God is wanting to turn our captivity.
God is wanting to destroy the yokes of financial bondage in our lives ! The reason much of the body of Christ is in debt and bondage is because it has become accepted.

But God is raising up a people in these last days who are declaring;

"NO! My God is turning my captivity,
    MY God wants me to be above and not beneath,
        THE HEAD and NOT THE TAIL,
            HE WANTS ME TO LEND TO MANY and borrow
            from none,

So I'm not going to PUT UP with scarcity, lack, and bondage because I Have a deliverer whose name is Jesus that delights in the prosperity of his servant ! Therefore no weapon or plan formed against me and my plan will prosper ! I will form a counter-plan. I will get tougher. I will persevere until I win !

The Bible's greatest example of a man who had a plan to counter the enemies' plan against him was Nehemiah. He rebuilt the wall in the midst of constant threat and intimidation by the enemies of Jerusalem but Nehemiah always made a plan to counter the enemies' plan and kept moving forward.

5. A Long term vision will help you overcome short term setbacks

So many times it seems as we press toward our goal we go three steps forward and two steps back. So what should we do when we encounter setbacks, even painful setbacks? Refuse to quit, somehow find the strength to go on and allow your long term vision to help you overcome short-term setbacks. Multinational corporations frequently have quarterly reports that are down in certain geographical sectors. At such times they keep their confidence buoyed by focusing on good reports in other sectors. Usually even in the midst of a setback something good is happening somewhere in your world. I started a church with one person in a living room and the church grew to about twenty people within two years. Then several key people made a group exodus from our infant church plant and our church was down to almost nothing. The stress of it caused my wife to break out in hives so badly that I had to send her to Korea to recover. Alone, abandoned, and seeing little hope I picked up a modern version of a verse in Roman's 16 which said, *God will come to the aid of those who refuse to quit.*

I didn't know if **anybody** would be there at the next Sunday service but I refused to quit. As I preached to an almost empty room a mountain man made his way into the service and tearfully rededicated his life to Christ. Every service for the next few months he would weep tears of thanksgiving at God's gracious work in his life through the church. I realized I had a choice, I could focus on the setback or I could look at this gentleman weeping in the glow of the new life Christ had given him. That man turned out to be an amazing pillar in the church for years to come; our beloved deacon Grizzly Al Kaikona. (They call him Grizzly Al because he had a business of taking rich easterners into the Grizzly infested mountains to teach them to live off the land with nothing but a flint and steel.)

As a church we've had several such setbacks but God keeps coming to the aid of those who refuse to quit. So focus on the rose not the thorn and that will help you find strength to keep a long term vision that will help you overcome short term setbacks.

6. Set goals and write the goals down

If we want to prosper we must plan and set goals; spiritual goals, financial goals, short term goals, long term goals, then write the goals down. Even finishing this book was a goal for me, if it hadn't been, I never would have finished.

A university study found that their alumni who wrote their goals down achieved 90% of their goals. Those who did not achieved 10% of their goals. There is power in having the goal written down.

Habakkuk 2:2 says *WRITE the vision down and make it plain on tablets so that he that reads it may run with it. Once your goals are written* you can prioritize your most important asset, time, thus enabling you to **run with it** not keep it on the back burner for five years.

At the writing down stage remember a plan is " a method for accomplishing an objective" which usually involves "a drawing or diagram showing the parts and details of a thing." We started our business, HuckleberryLand, in the carport of my trailer which was one block back from the highway. God blessed the work of our hands and we expanded but we did not own the piece of land that was between us and the highway so our tourist business could have easily been blocked had the owner of that piece built upon it. Because of our "land-locked" status I was looking for a piece of highway frontage I could purchase in order to relocate. My finances told me I could barely afford the smallest, worst piece I could find but then God spoke to me through a verse he often speaks to me through; Jeremiah 33:3 Call unto me and I will answer you and show you great and mighty things you know not of. I declared a short fast and called on God. I was then clearing my yard of some rocks before mowing and I threw the rocks onto the large field which was between my business and the highway. The Holy Spirit said, "don't do that", in my mind I knew God was right because throwing rocks there was not being a good neighbor, but to my surprise the Holy Spirit finished his sentence, "because you are going to own that piece of land and when you do you will have to pick the rocks back up !" Something clicked in my spirit and within a few days a realtor came and put a for sale sign on the land which was 10 prime lots with 300 feet of frontage. The price of $145,000 seemed way out of reach but I conceived a creative offer involving owner financing and GOD CAME THROUGH ! (Not without a lot of work and years of paying it off on our part but he made the impossible possible.) So many times you do the natural and God will do the supernatural.

Paying the land off took about ten years, meanwhile we really wanted to expand our business and move it closer to the highway. It never happened partly because I never made a "drawing or diagram showing the details" of the new facility. In early 2008 I was preaching this series at our church and when I was on O, seizing the opportunity, I felt convicted because I had this great land but was not seizing the potential it carried. I got up at about 3:33 A.M. feeling convicted by my own sermon and I began pencilling out a feasible drawing and diagram of the new building together with a "means to accomplishing the objective" in terms of refinancing my home and acreage in order to afford it. By the time the night was over my heavenly Father said he'd back me by quickening Psalm 20 to my spirit, "May he send you help from the sanctuary and grant you support from Zion. May he give you the desire of your heart and make all your plans succeed."

In the morning I shocked my dear wife again with another of God's 3:33 great and mighty plans. She was scared at the magnitude of the plan, over 5,400 square feet on a single story, so she laid down some practical objectives concerning my health while I was to construct it, I agreed to her wise guidelines, then she gave me the go ahead to build. I walked out to the property and tried to figure out where to start... There was two feet of snow on the ground and doubts were insisting I could never get it done in time for the upcoming season. Every nerve in my being wanted to press the abort button but a bald eagle soared strangely above the property which gave me a sense that God would help me. I ordered the heavy equipment and dug the huge hole for the foundation. I poured the footings myself in bad weather but once that was done the fear and trembling in my mind left because I knew I was committed.

A robust carpenter came to help me but then he vanished. I found him in jail for DUI and led him to Christ through the plexiglas in the visitor's booth. After praying the tough dude said, "I'm shaking." He held steady and we worked like possessed men. I took twelve days off to do a large scale crusade in the Philippines, cared for the church as it's pastor, and maintained domestic tranquility while managing to complete the building in 3 1/2 months in time for the 2008 tourist season. NOW THAT'S GOD ! But he never would have moved if I didn't make a "drawing or diagram showing the details" and conceive a "means to accomplishing an objective". God is a man with a plan, how about you ?

I heard Joel Osteen speak on this topic saying we need to make a plan to get out of debt. He said if you had $5,000 on your credit card and made the minimum payment of $22.00 per month it would take you 86 1/2 years to pay it off and you would have payed $38,000 interest. But he stated that the average couple in his church who starts seeing a financial counsellor and develops a plan can be debt free in 3-5 years with the exception of their house mortgage. Then once they are they can make one extra payment a year and knock 8 years off their 30 year mortgage.

Make a plan, write down the "drawing or diagram showing the details" and conceive a "means to accomplishing an objective". YOU DO THE NATURAL and God will do the supernatural. He will "send you help from the sanctuary and make all your plans succeed."

7. Once you plan, prune; re-evaluate as plans unfold.

A plan shows you what you should do, in doing so it also shows you what you should not do. Paul the apostle's God given plan and ambition caused him to shy away from other good ministries; *It has always been my ambition to preach the gospel where Christ was not known so that I would not be building on someone else's foundation. THIS IS WHY I have often been hindered from coming to you.* Romans 15: v.20 v.22

Once you know what you are called to do and make a plan to fulfill that calling then you also know what you are not called to do and you should prune some of those activities off so you can give yourself more fully to the plan; I am the true vine and my father is the gardener. He cuts off every branch in me that bears no fruit, while every branch that does bear fruit he prunes so it will be even more fruitful. John 15:1-2 Light is good but focused light can form a laser beam that will even cut through steel. By re-evaluating and pruning we can stay focused and do a few things well.

My father had a successful tourist business which had great growth potential. Instead of focusing on the branch that was making him money, the Huckleberry Jam and Pie factory and the gift shop, he started a vocational college and a summer

45

playhouse. The college and playhouse were expensive to start and expensive to run and began sucking the fiscal health out of his empire. When a difficult season came the lucrative tourist business could not sustain the college and playhouse and he lost everything to the bank. A couple bought his operation from the bank, closed the playhouse and college, then expanded the "goose that laid the golden egg" and produced an extremely profitable business. Re-evaluate and do the pruning based on fruitfulness, give attention to the branches that are producing and scrap the ones which are not. Sometimes we as a church will try new directions and programs. If it isn't fruitful we bury it in an unmarked grave. If the horse dies, dismount!

Many times a plan will push us in a new direction which requires some time to develop to the point that it will sustain us financially. At such times of transition don't violate Tarzan's first rule of the jungle; don't let go of the vine you are holding till you have a firm grasp on the next vine. (Prune carefully and don't prune too soon.)

I, by nature, enjoy a variety of activities so I must constantly re-evaluate and keep myself focused since time is valuable and limited.

Chapter Review for Plan;

Plan; a method for accomplishing an objective. Usually a plan involves "a drawing or diagram showing the parts and details of a thing."

The remote is in you hand. The decision path and plan you make now you will be watching 5 years from now on the screen of your life.

1. God has a plan, to prosper you, to give you a future and a hope Jeremiah 29:11

2. God will make known those plans to you. The spirit will put the plans into your mind 1 Chronicles 28:11-12

3. Establish the plan through counsel.
 a. a multitude
 b. your own heart

4. Your enemy has a plan to contain you so you'd better prepare a plan to counter his resistance.
a. persevere until you win/ Nehemiah

5. A long term vision will help you overcome short term setbacks

6. Set goals and write the goals down.

7. Once you plan, prune; re-evaluate as plans unfold.   As you prune don't violate Tarzan's first rule of the jungle; don't let go of the first vine till you have firm grasp of the next one.

To go forward in total life prosperity requires a breaking out of the mindset that anchored you to a life of lack.

All thought patterns are set in stone which is precisely why they call it a "mind-set". If our mind-set is wrong, then we will self-sabotage when it comes time to break out of our old thinking pattern and break into the new. In short we are unable to reach our destiny because our mind will not allow it. (#FN Sabotage Insight publishing group. Mike Connaway C. 2003.)

Our thought patterns get set in stone and become a mind set. When we are young perhaps our thoughts are more flexible and are still forming like green concrete. But once we are older many of our thoughts have become firmly set and it will take intentional work on our mindset in order to change.

Many have made financial status a moral issue. People start out with a desire to do better in life and do more for God but somewhere along the line they hit obstacles which confine and limit them. Rather than overcoming the obstacles many let their life be defined by the limitations. Next they create a moral framework to justify their position, "I'm just the blue-collar hard working backbone of America." Some go so far as to consciously or subconsciously label people with more money as morally inferior; "I work for mine but those doctors, lawyers and preachers just prey on us honest folk." Now their mind set is further cemented by creating a moral framework that commends poverty and condemns having money. There are many supporting actors in this caste system that binds people to poverty; family members who judge and label you if you begin doing better than the rest, friends who also think rich people are unethical snobs, perhaps a political party that has a socialistic influence which teaches we should all reach a certain economic status but no more, maybe a world view that says poor mother earth is just about depleted of resources so you had better live on as little as you can. All these can be like threads which weave a fabric that can keep us anchored to poverty. In the midst of this house of thoughts addictions to beer, pot, tobacco,TV, and porn can crop up to drain away time and money and further ensnare a person in poverty. So to prosper we must first RID ourselves of a poverty mentality by breaking out of the old mind set ON PURPOSE. Say aloud, "on purpose."

Montana is usually ranked in the bottom 5 states in the union regarding per capita income. The "canyon" area I was raised in is one of the more depressed regions of Montana. My father was an intelligent entrepeneur so I didn't grow up hangin' with too many of the economically depressed residents.   I was popular, smart and did sports. But in high school I rebelled against the shallowness I saw in the popular school cliques and I joined the hard-up, hard partying clans of Martin City Montana. I experienced first hand the factors which keep people poor.

It's been said, and I believe it, that if communism had it's way and all wealth was evenly redistributed within a short while those who had been rich would be rich again and those who had been poor would be poor again because the mindset and habits that make for poverty or wealth had not been changed. I found pride to be one of the gatekeepers in the jail of poverty. There is a wholesome type of satisfying pride in one's country, church, or accomplishment, but there is also a harmful pride which is arrogant and unteachable; "I know it all don't try tellin' me what to do !" The party crowd I ran with had this unwholesome brand of pride which was actually proud of the poverty. We were like "men from snowy river" who eeked out a living from a cold rugged land. The mindset was; "we work in the woods earning every dollar we make. We spend most of what we make on drink and drugs on the weekend. We're tough as iron from carrying a chain saw all day and we could bust your head in. We're broke and proud of it." (I am in no way speaking down at hard working blue collar people because I'm a blue collar guy that's worked hard and done well. The Bible commends rolling up our sleeves and working hard. I'm not taking aim at a certain social class I'm explaining a specific mindset I encountered that held people in bondage.)

Those were the guys I hung with and pretty soon I became like them, tattered jean clothing, loggin' boots, Stihl chain saw, barbell polished biceps. A lot of the guys in the 'South Fork Saloon" or "Packers Roost" had a six shooter on their side, including me, and weren't afraid to use it. When the bars closed the fights would start. After the South Fork closed one night one of our gang, Daryl, got miffed at Bill and not only beat him up but got him down on the icy street and repeatedly kicked him in the head. Once a Native American we were pickin' on came runnin' out of the bar after us with a big metal pipe hollering his war cry! Another time two clans took sides and started a shootout in the streets of Martin City that lasted till 4 am. The next morning the headline read; "WILD WEST REVISITED". Even the night Jesus began getting my attention four loggers surrounded me in the middle of main street in Whitefish, MT. and one had a 357 magnum pointed at my head !

50

The whole lifestyle was steeped in pride. Not only the pride that produced fist fights but a pride that held people to an inadequate salary, and a lifestyle that was devoid of creativity and advancement - all in the name of being the tough, hard workin', canyon people.

I was stayin' in an apartment across from the bar with Roger, a wiry guy who was locally famous for whippin' 3 or 4 men at the same time in the Deer Lick Saloon, and Donny, an irish kid that had a wall full of boxing trophy's.   One Sunday morning I woke up on my old sofa with the usual throbbing hangover. I didn't remember much about the night before but did remember puking till blood came out.   Our apartment reeked like old beer and when my buddys got up we all cracked a beer to get rid of our hangover. We were so broke that all of us together couldn't put together enough money for breakfast, so Donny looked under the sink and found old potatoes, from the last renter, that had 10 inch sprouts coming off them in every direction.   He sliced them up and made them into hash-browns and that was our breakfast!   I had a smile on my face like everyone else but when I closed the bathroom door I looked at myself in the mirror and said to myself, Buddy Willows you're gonna be dead if you keep this up, find a way out of this lifestyle!   I had no idea the way out was named Jesus, but within several months he became the way, the truth and the life for me.... the way OUT of that destructive lifestyle.

Looking back I find it incredulous that the devil can make people proud of such insanity, but the pride even birthed songs that championed the lifestyle, songs like, "Wasted Days and Wasted Nights", "Wastin' away again in Margaritaville", "We Don't Need No Education," or another one I liked "Gonna Lay Around the Shanty and Get a Good Buzz

On". The pride and the music re-enforced the mindset which held many in poverty and addiction. I believe poverty is a spirit and carries a smell.... No wonder Jesus said the spirit of the Lord had anointed him to preach good news to the poor; "poor man, you don't have to be poor any longer because I the anointed one have come to destroy that yoke." (I'm not saying everyone who is financially challenged has "a demon of poverty". There are people who don't have much money and are keeping themselves clean and making a difference where they are but there are also those who are oppressed by a poverty that you can smell which makes their daughters sell themselves for sex and their homes a habitation of hell.)

When I came to Christ and began hearing God's word concerning prosperity being the reward of the righteous I had to RID my mind of years of "stinkin' thinkin" before I could enter in to the prosperity which God's word spoke of. I had to dump years of being programmed for poverty by the thoughts and the music of my geographical region. I didn't have any religious programming to undo because I was a total stranger to religion but many believers also have to RID themselves of religious traditions and false teachings in order to begin experiencing God's best. Perhaps religious stinkin' thinkin' is the hardest of all to be RID of.

Proverbs 23:7 says "as a man thinketh in his heart so is he." That means what you have been thinking is what you are today. It means what you are thinking today is what you will become tomorrow, because as a man thinketh in his heart so is he. So before you can prosper you must rid yourself of stinkin' thinkin' and a poverty mentality. The only way you can do that is to get a check up from the neck up then begin renewing your mind to the truth of God's word.

Historians have noted that throughout history people have subconsciously become LIKE the gods they worshipped. If their gods were confused and chaotic they were that way too. If their gods were stern and merciless they were like that as a culture. People tend to live up to, or down to their image of God. That's why Christianity with the true God of love; Jesus Christ coming to serve, to forgive, and to give his life on the cross is the most powerful force in the universe. It gives all mankind a wonderful, forgiving God to emulate.

In the same way if we think God is El Cheepo we will live like that. I'm happy to be a bearer of good news to you today, God's name is not El Cheepo it is El Shaddai.

And when Abram was ninety years old and nine, the Lord appeared to Abram, and said to him, I am the Almighty God: walk before me, and be thou perfect. Genesis 17:1 KJV.

When the Lord appeared to Abraham, what he actually said in Hebrew was, I am El Shaddai..." El Shaddai is one of seven covenant names through which God revealed himself to Israel. In Hebrew El Shaddai means " The All-Sufficient One," or "The God who is more than enough."

The translators of the King James translated El Shaddai as "Almighty God." I like that. If He is the All Sufficient One, then he is Almighty: "the God who is more than enough." (El Shaddai, Kenneth E. Hagan, C.1980 Rhema Bible Church.)

I like that EL Shaddai, the God who is More than Enough ! In 2002 one of my congregation had a bad heart attack and was expected to die. As He was lying on his hospital bed he was looking up at the white square ceiling tile when suddenly the tile faded and the light of God's glory appeared. God spoke to him, "**I am** El Shaddai and **you are** going to be OK !" Within a day or two he packed his stuff and left the hospital as a walking miracle! **El Shaddai** is **the God who is more than enough** for whatever situation you may be facing !

Some of us have allowed religion to paint God as El Cheepo not El Shaddai ! Because of this we can hardly see El Shaddai in the pages of the Bible. So we're going to take a short walk through the Bible that will help RID us of a poverty mentality; The Bible begins with Adam being provided every conceivable blessing and advantage. The word of God ends with God providing his people a city whose walls are made of precious stone and whose streets are made of translucent gold. They are not paved with gold, they are gold all the way through. In between Genesis and Revelation we find "Proverbs", a how to manual on prosperity. The word of God reveals a God of abundance and a people of plenty;

Genesis 1:27-28 So God created man in his own image, in the image of God created he him; male and female created he them, (male and female not Adam and Steve.) And God blessed them, and God said unto them. Be fruitful and multiply, and replenish the earth, and subdue it; and have dominion over the fish of the sea, and over the fowl of the air, and over every living thing that moveth upon the earth. KJV.

So the first thing God did after creating man is bless them. His heart toward his man is revealed immediately. He desires to bless his man. Notice also that the word says he blessed them. The blessing was not just the dominion mandate. Before he ever gave them dominion the text says he blessed them. The word *"Bless"* in this context means *empower to prosper*. **So first of all God conferred upon them an empowerment to prosper. HE BLESSED THEM then he spoke over them their job description** of how they were to take dominion in the earth but it is significant that before he outlined their task he first empowered them to fulfill it.   (Just like Jesus did in Acts 1, He said YOU SHALL RECEIVE POWER when the Holy Ghost comes upon you and you shall be my witnesses first in Jerusalem, then in Judea and Samaria and even unto the ends of the earth !   (First the power then the job description.)

Say, "I am empowered to prosper!"

Say, "I am empowered to take dominion in the earth!"

Say, "I am empowered to take the gospel to _____" (your city)

"and to the cities and reservations of _____ "

(the outlying towns)

Say,

"I am empowered to take the gospel into the ends of the earth !"

Then as we progress through scripture God finds this normal dude called Abram. The only thing he had going for him was he had a stunningly attractive wife and he possessed the heart of a father ..... who would carefully instruct his children after him.   It was for that reason God zeroed in on him......   HEY ABRAM ! (Abram looks up)

"Leave your country, your people, and your father's household and go to the land I will show you."   In other words before you can prosper you must RID yourself of some baggage, **you must CUT the umbilical cord that held you to a mindset of poverty !** Then he pronounced four blessings,

1. I will make you into a great nation and I will bless you.

2. I will make your name great and you will be a blessing.

3. I will bless those who bless you and whoever curses you I will curse; and

4. All peoples on earth will be blessed through you. Genesis 12:1-3

Once again before God even properly introduced himself to his man he is doing what ? He is blessing him ! Only 12 chapters into the Bible and we see two cases of God blessing his man before even introducing himself. That should tell us folks that the very nature and CORE of the one we serve is to be a blesser ! That is why it is such blasphemy to say God *damn* it ! Because God is not a damner, *God is and forever will be a blesser not a damner !* Well he's going to damn some people to hell pastor ! No he's not, he so loved the world that he gave his only son that whosoever believes shall not perish but have eternal life. If you reject that unbelievable gift YOU are choosing hell !! God is not damning you.

So God is the blesser, and he blessed Abram. Those four blessings are not just for the Old testament Patriarch. Galatians 3:13-14 asserts that by becoming a curse on the tree Christ redeemed us from the curse of the law IN ORDER THAT **the Blessing given to Abraham** might come upon the gentiles through Christ Jesus. The four fold blessing bestowed on Abraham didn't stop with Abraham. If you are a gentile like me the word says the blessing has come upon you through Christ Jesus. Say I HAVE THE BLESSING !

I am arranging for my son Josiah to go to Chicago next month to check out a college he is interested in. As we were eating at a fine area restaurant named Wendy's (sometimes you have to eat at those kind of restaurants to afford college,) I told Josiah, I bought your ticket to Chicago Josiah and I'm having you taken to Wheaton College in a limousine. The rest of the family exclaimed, no Dad you're joking, you are not having him go in a limo ! I said, yes I am, no kid of mine is going to ride in a normal old taxi !   I'm just an earthly father and that's how I feel about my children and the bible says how much more will your father in heaven give good things to those who ask him ! The white limo had him stylin' in Chicago !

After Abram went through the rid stage and cut the umbilical cord to his old mindset which for him required a physical separation from the kinfolk and geographical region that defined him. God told him I'm going to change your name from Abram to Abra HAM. The Hebrew word for Spirit is RUAHHH. And in Anaheim Benny Hinn taught us that HAMM is a form of RUAHHH and that the HAMM was God empowering Abram by his Spirit. As I stated earlier the word bless when it comes from God is an empowerment to prosper so God is taking a very normal Arab named Abram and is emPOWERing him with the RUAHH of heaven ! Then to forever brand him as a heaven empowered man he incorporates the word for Spirit into his name; Abra HAM ! From that moment onward Abram will remember that God's super has come upon his natural !

Don't YOU FORGET either;
    God has called you,
        God has filled you with His Spirit,
        God has commissioned you,
            and empowered YOU to prosper !
He may be Abra HAM, but I'm JamesHAM, not James the Ham, but James the empowered, and you are ____HAM. When you go through life remembering THAT then you will

say with Jeremiah, Aw Lord God thou hast made the heavens and the earth by thy great power,
and NOTHING is too difficult for thee !

God made Abram a supernatural man. Some people act superwierd when the Holy Ghost comes upon them, but I believe God is wanting to raise up super*natural* people. My board members, Cary and Wendy Swanson from B.C. are just fun people that climb mountains all over the world yet as they cruise around and joke and laugh there is a powerful anointing on their life. They are super*natural* people. My son Abe is another example. As I tuck him into bed sometimes I say Abra and then I let out a soft breathy HAAAMMMM ! gently into his ear. He loves it and laughs so hard as I do it. I am consciously giving him a father's blessing as I do it. He's just a fun popular kid but he's a supernatural kid too. He is a touchdown making machine in football, one year he averaged 13.6 yards per carry ! I took him to one of the most competitive football camps in the country (Offense-Defense Atlanta) and he proved in the 40 yard dash competition that he was the fastest 10 year old in the camp and one of the parents told me their kid was ranked in the top 100 fastest in the nation. By the end of camp he'd won an award allowing us to go anywhere in the USA for the next camp for free. (a $730.00 value.....You should write a book; it's another great place to brag about your kids!) Expect God's Abrahamic blessing to make you super*natural* not super *wierd*. (I think Abraham's wife Sarah had a super*natural* beauty upon her that made her a babe without equal !)

Next we see Israel released from Egypt and God caused the Egyptians to be favorably disposed toward them and they gave them items of silver and gold so that God's people were laden with valuables as they left Egypt. Many preachers preach Pharaoh as a type of satan, the passover lamb as a type of Jesus, the passing through the red sea as a type of the deliverance that comes to us through the blood of Jesus but my friends this preacher isn't going to leave out the part about our salvation including the wealth of the sinner being laid up for the just ! When God redeemed Israel he also made them rich and there was not a feeble person among them.

As you continue through God's word you come to 1 Kings 7 where a whole city was in severe famine and eating pigeon poop. (Because of disobedience) But one word from the prophet Elisha and the siege was completely broken by four lowly lepers. Don't let the world talk you into recessions and embargo's and shortages, one word from God can change your situation overnight. Time would fail me to tell of David as a type of the messiah who greatly expanded the holy nations borders and provided truckloads of gold to build the temple. Or of his son who asked for wisdom and was given riches and honor as well so much so that during Solomon's reign silver was considered of little value because gold was so common.

The Psalms are full of the prosperity message; Ps.37:4 Delight yourself in the Lord and he will give you the desires of your heart, Psalm 128 1-2 Blessed are all who fear the Lord, who walk in his ways. You will eat the fruit of your labor; blessings and prosperity will be yours. Psalm 112 Blessed is the man who fears the Lord,..... wealth and riches are in his house and his righteousness endures forever. Psalm 19 says God's words are perfect and righteous altogether then declares that by them is your servant warned; and in keeping them there is **great reward**.

Perhaps the psalms are summarized when David exclaimed; "the Lord is my shepherd I shall not want!" Some preach that God will only do something about your needs, but David knew a shepherd who also did something about his wants. But Pastor I have enemies, that's OK, David said the table your shepherd prepares for you is right in the presence of your enemies.

The book of proverbs is a veritable how to guide about prosperity claiming that prosperity is the reward of the righteous. (Misfortune pursues the sinner but prosperity is the reward of the righteous.) Proverbs 13:21

Isaiah declares that God's people will receive a double portion in the land and that aliens will work our fields because we will be called priests of the Lord.

The Old Covenant concludes with Malachi declaring that God will open the heavens and pour out a blessing that cannot be contained upon the obedient tither. Don't miss the blessing associated with tithing to your local church. Hebrews 7 says in the Old Covenant men who died received the tithe but in our dispensation "He that liveth forever" (Jesus Christ) receives our tithe. (Who is our New Covenant High Priest in the order of Melchizadek.)

But pastor you skipped Job's story about how God took all his stuff away. First of all God didn't take his stuff, Satan did, because Job opened the door to the one who comes to "steal, kill, and destroy" by giving in to fear; Job said, "that which I so greatly feared has come upon me." Secondly the entire ordeal lasted 6-9 months and when it was over God gave him double for his trouble till he was the Bill Gates of the near East.

Jesus came on the scene turned water into wine, 5 loaves and 2 fish into a feast that fed 5,000, and promised his faithful followers 100 fold multiplication in this lifetime for homes and fields they had sown into his kingdom. (with persecutions)

Paul shares in Corinthians that the measure we sow financially will be the measure we reap financially and assures the generous giver that "God is able to make all grace (every favor and earthly blessing) come to you in abundance, so that you may always and under all circumstances and whatever the need be self sufficient. (possessing enough to require no aid or financial support and furnished in abundance for every good work and charitable donation.) 2 Corinthians 9:8 Amplified Version

The New Testament also teaches that we are now adopted sons of El Shaddai and joint heirs with Jesus of all that his household offers. I think the reason the older son got so angry when the prodigal came home is that the father re-instated his inheritance by giving him the family ring. (Remember the scene in "Ben-Hur" when Arius was adopting Judah the culmination was the giving of the ring which would be used as a seal to conduct business in the name of Arius.) In the same way Jesus gave us his name of authority to use in prayer.

Is there sacrifice and a call to self denial in the New Testament ? Absolutely, but even the sacrifices made are rewarded both according to Jesus and according to Paul. And the denying of self Jesus calls us to is such that when we lose our life for his sake and for the gospel we really FIND life.

I think of Jerry Savelle who resisted the call of God for years because he loved cars and owned a struggling paint and body shop.

He then finally surrendered to God's call on his life to preach and went through several lean years but today Jerry owns numerous classic corvettes and hosts a yearly "Thunder over Texas" car and motorcycle rally where a thousand people received Christ last year. Yes there was a time of sacrificing the vocation that was dear to him but God multiplied everything Jerry gave up a hundredfold and gave him the joy of seeing it all used to the glory and advancement of God's kingdom. OH this makes me want to give something up for the gospel ! The author has sacrificed guitars for the gospel and today I have two fine guitars.

Hopefully the scriptures I've shared will help transform your image of God from El Cheepo to El Shaddai.

The two best ways to renew your mind are; **1. God's word** and faith filled preaching/teaching of His Word. **2. Music**

Psalm 1:1-3 As you meditate in his word day and night whatsoever your hands find to do will prosper. Joshua 1:8 Don't let the word depart from your mouth then you will make your way prosperous and have good success.

Meditate means to muse and to mutter--to not let the word depart from your mouth. Elmer Fudd knew what it was to meditate. As he walked through the woods he muttered, "that darn rabbit, eatin all my carrots,I'll fix that wabbit this time!" What are you muttering ? Muttering doubt and unbelief kept Israel out of the promised land. Had they reversed the words and began muttering how if God is for them who could be against them HOW QUICKLY God would have defeated their adversaries !   Meditate also means to muse... to muse...muse ic. Music causes thoughts and themes to get stuck in your mind. That's why I guard my mind like a pitbull guards a bone. I would no sooner listen to a worldly non-christian song than I would eat poison on purpose. Ya but pastor I like that secular song, the band is real good. It's not the big things that separate the winners from the losers. It's not the big things that separate those who prosper from those who win some and lose some. It's the DETAILS ! And Lyrics that do not glorify God and bring wholesome thoughts into your head will never bring you the same results as music that is uplifting and helps you muse on the word.

Much of my pre-conversion drug and sex lifestyle was anchored and encouraged by the music I listened to. From Clapton's "Cocaine," to Van Halen's sex ballads and "Runnin With the Devil." Two weeks after I became a christian a theif broke into my sports car and stole all my cassette tapes. My buddy and I were so ticked we tracked them for blocks in the snow but later I thanked God because I realized that music had to go if I was going to grow as a believer.

Just as poverty needs songs to reinforce it's mindset, songs like "wasted days and wasted nights," if you will get music that fills you with faith, God's word, psalms of His goodness, worship.... you will find the new mindset needed comes rather effortlessly because that is the beauty of music it makes it easy to remember the desired content.

I was El Cheepo son of El Cheepo at one stage of my life then God began doing things that showed me what El Shaddai was like. I married the daughter of a famous South Korean movie director. Jaekyung's Dad came and wanted to buy us a refrigerator. I immediately suggested we buy one used out of the Mountain Trader. (The weekly newspaper where people here sell things, it's like the Montana man's bible.) Oh no they want to go to the appliance store. At the store I gravitate toward the clearance models and suggest a nice $395.00 Fridge. Meanwhile they are ignoring me and asking the salesman about the $1400.00 Amana and he bought it for her without even blinking! Now I call him El Shaddad, His love for his daughter helped RID me of a poverty mentality. Jesus once said, if you *earthly fathers* know how to give good gifts to your children, though you are evil, *compared to the heavenly father,* how much more will your Father in heaven give good gifts to those who ask him. Matthew 7:11

One final story of how God helped me out of a poverty mindset;
As we were leaving for Jamaica to be missionaries, we had no way in the natural to see ourselves into a vehicle once we got there. We asked God what we should do about this predicament and the Holy Spirit instructed me to call Korn Buick in Kalispell. I asked the Holy Spirit who I should ask for and he told me DAN. I finally got up the nerve to call, it somehow helped that the number was 7777, "is there a Dan who works there I asked ?" Yes one in service and one who is the owner. I made an appointment to see the owner, got dressed in my suit, and Jaekyung and I came into the fine dealership and met the tall distinguished owner in his office. It helped a little that his office displayed a plaque that said, "Trust in the Lord with all your heart and lean not on your own understanding." I was very nervous and asked for a glass of water as I killed time with small talk. Finally I got up the nerve and told him why I'd come, "we are missionaries leaving for foreign soil and we don't have a vehicle nor money to buy one and will need one. In asking God about my dilema God told me to come talk to you about it." Now it was his turn to get nervous and fidget. Nothing seemed to come of it except that we became friends and they had us over for dinner.

After six months in Jamaica our only bicycle was stolen and we needed transportation desperately. I'd scraped together $3,000. and was preparing to buy a junky old yellow Corolla held together by bondo. (Cars were expensive there) God slammed the door in my face and no matter how I pushed and connived the deal would not go through.

The devil told me, "see how mean God is you gave up good cars to be a missionary and now you have to walk. He just wants you to be poor forever." Had I believed those lies I would have stayed afoot but I started walking in faith and declaring that my God was meeting my need for a vehicle ! In a few weeks time we were forced to go to Miami to renew our visa and before departing some money came for a vehicle including a large check from The Dan Korn family. In Miami we purchased a nearly new pickup that was a class act and would have cost three times as much in Jamaica. When God closes a door look for him to open a window. God closed the door on a yellow lemon and opened a door of great blessing ! And we were blessed to be a blessing because when we left we blessed a Christian boy's home with it. Walking with my good father helped me RID myself of a poverty mentality as I opened my heart and mind to His higher ways.

Prayer; Forgive me for groveling like a worm when I can soar like an eagle.

Confession; I can serve God better rich than I can broke.
(Dr. Creflo Dollar)

O. pportunity must be seized   Chapter 7

If you desire to prosper in your calling, in your business and in your life in general, you must **recognize opportunity when it comes and be willing to seize the opportunity.** Say it, *"Seize the opportunity;"*

1. Recognize Opportunity; A favorable combination of circumstances, time and place. A chance for advancement. A set of circumstances that makes it possible to do something.

2. Be willing to seize the opportunity

Paul saw an opportunity he speaks of in 1 Corinthians 16:9 A great door and effective is opened unto me, and there are many adversaries.

Amplified; A wide door of effective service has been opened unto me, one great and promising...

So Paul saw a great wide door of opportunity opened unto him, yet with that opportunity came adversity and challenge.

"The reason many people miss opportunities is because they, opportunities, come wearing overalls and they look like work." Thomas Edison

Many people want the success other people have had but they are not willing to do what others have done to seize the opportunity. But Paul was not that kind of guy, he was a realist, He understood full well that this opportunity was dressed in work clothes. This opportunity came packaged in adversity. Yet Paul didn't vasilate, he understood full well a very important principle, opportunities must be seized ! When Paul, in a dream, saw the man from Macedonia beckon to him for help the word says HE LEFT AT ONCE to seize this opportunity for service !

I remember when the iron curtain dropped and after 70 years of intense oppression and persecution, Russia opened its' door to missionaries. We dropped all our plans, packed up Josiah, who was 1 1/2 at the time... talk about a door of opportunity with some adversity, try going thousands of miles by plane and train with a 1 1/2 year old. We seized that favorable combination of circumstances, time, and place and went to assist a church in discipling converts through a 3 month long Bible School which we held in a hall that seated over 200. We spoke to the city of over a million on TV, discipled about 200 new converts 3 times a week, led 200 people to Christ, saw suicides cancelled, watched God heal many people, and beheld the church we were assisting grow from 300 to 600 that summer. Today it's one of the larger churches in Russia with over 2,000 members. Although I have returned to Russia twice in subsequent years none of the harvests equalled that first trip. Why ? Because it was a favorable combination of circumstances, time and place which had to be SEIZED !

Seize means "to take possession of suddenly and by force as by attack or strike."

This reminds me of MT. 11:12; From the days of John the Baptist until now, the kingdom of heaven suffereth violence and the violent take it by force. KJV   Even the Kingdom of God must be seized violently !

Another definition of seize is "to take an opportunity eagerly and decisively." Some believers can't even decide wether they want fries or a baked potatoe at the fricken restaurant but this Bible is full of people who seized their opportunity eagerly and decisively;

While others waited and wondered Peter left his nets and his estate and followed Christ.
Elisha burned the 12 oxen and followed Elijah.
When offered the princess and tax exemption David ran to the battle lines to meet Goliath.
When Mary was told she would birth the messiah she immediately told Gabriel, "be it unto me according to thy word." She didn't say, "come back in a week after I pray about it."

Others in scripture missed opportunities; Jehoash was told by Elisha to strike the ground with arrows. He struck only three times and the prophet was angry and told him, you should have struck the ground six times then you would have completely destroyed Aram. Gehazi missed the chance to be the next prophet. Jesus told the goats, "I was hungry and you fed me not." Some, according to God's word, will miss the ultimate opportunity, heaven !

We all miss opportunities but don't you miss that one, don't put off receiving Jesus Christ as your Lord and Savior ! Seize that opportunity !

Some people want to make sure all the conditions are perfect before they will act; they want to do it next year, but opportunities don't always wait for the faint-hearted, slow to move, or for cowards. Think of Thomas Edison; In 1854 the schoolmaster told him he was weak in the head - so in all his life he only received 3 months of school. At age 12 he needed money for his experiments so he began selling newspapers and snacks in a passenger train. He had no time for his experiments so he did them in the baggage car of the train. He needed more money for science books so he bought an old printing press, put it in the baggage car with his experiments, and began writing and printing his own newspaper - even though he couldn't spell. One day as he was trying to get on the train with his hands full he was stumbling and a well meaning gent pulled him up on the train by his ear. Something snapped and from then on he couldn't hear properly. No schooling, no investors, no hearing but at age 29, with people laughing in his face, he opened his "Invention Factory" at Menlo Park, New Jersey. He'd sleep only four hours a day as he busied himself with his inventions. He said, "I have so much to do, and life is so short. I've got to hustle." While others were waiting for "opportunity to knock" Edison seized his opportunity. (**The Story of Thomas Alva Edison,** Inventor, Scholastic Inc., Margaret Davidson)

Henry Ford said that when he was a very young boy, his mother taught him that life would present many opportunities, but it would take self-discipline, courage, and perseverance to make those opportunities a reality. Think of that statement in relationship to your situation; life will present many opportunities but it will take self-discipline, courage, and perseverance to make those opportunities a reality.

3 Qualities needed to seize an opportunity,

1. Discipline

Discipline is the ability to adhere to order and training.
Some charismatics don't like hearing about discipline. They want to "let go and let God" but the Lord who called them called them to be a disciple. The root word for discipline is disciple... one who has entered into training. Jesus' followers

were called disciples, they had accepted Jesus as their mentor and were engaged in regular training that was causing them to be so much like him that they were later called Christians. Or those who were like Christ. So God is calling us to be **disciple**ined ones. (My mentor says **I do need to** let go and let God sometimes, He calls me "one jacked up dude," Ha!")

I was admiring our deacon's growing physique and asked him how much weight training he did daily to produce that kind of results. He replied, "one or two hours." I wanted the three minute miracle, or the pill that produces, but the truth is that what REALLY produces is discipline, the ability to adhere to order and training. It will take discipline to make your opportunity a reality.

Keeman Wilson the founder of the Holiday Inns, was once asked what the key to his success was. He replied, I've worked half days all my life, so I guess my advice to anyone who wants to be successful is to just work half days the rest of your life. It doesn't really matter which half you work, the first 12 hours, or the last 12 hours. Ya but pastor I don't have a job. Work 12 hours a day putting out resume's and knocking on doors you will soon have one.

The book of proverbs talks about the exact opposite, As a door turns on it's hinges so a sluggard turns on his bed. The sluggard says, "there is a lion in the road, a fierce lion is roaming the streets." So rather than work half days and succeed like Keeman Wilson the sluggard turns on his bed. And rather than seizing the opportunities life presents the sluggard can list all the reasons why he or she should not take action; the economy is unstable, it's the last days we must prepare to hide in the hills, there is a lion in the streets. (Seizing God Given Opportunities, Harrison House, Jerry Savelle)

I'm sad to say that many preachers and so called prophets are the ones responsible for creating these lions in people's thinking. Do you remember the Y2K bug.... at the stroke of midnight 2000 the banking system would collapse, electricity would go off, even our cars and microwaves would no longer work because they are ALL tied in to computer chips which are about to cause everything to FREAK OUT.

That lion in the streets kept many believers cautious, it hindered them from seizing opportunities. The preachers and the prophets were the only ones who seized the opportunity because their fear producing books sold millions. In the midst of all that a wise man of God named Happy Caldwell had many experts on his TV show and in his pulpit telling people "NO it's going to be OK," the electric company came out, banking professionals spoke on his show. Still his congregation was skittish so Pastor Caldwell held a big service on New Years eve. About 4 minutes to 12:00AM his wife was singing a lovely song and the mic went dead and all the lights in the building went off.... Happy shouted out, "this is not Y2K !" Then his wife just kept right on singin'... It turned out a drunk down the road had hit a telephone poll and knocked the power off !

The sluggard says there is a *lion in the streets*. But don't prescribe to *the lion in the streets* theology. If you've already prescribed to it CANCEL your subscription.

Begin to walk on the more sure word of prophecy !
    Which says God delights in the prosperity of his servant !
Begin to walk on the more sure word of prophecy !
    Which says I've never seen the righteous forsaken or their seed begging bread.

Begin to walk on the more sure word of prophecy !

Which says that those who trust in the LORD are like a tree planted by the water, which, even in a year of drought or famine, NEVER FAILS TO PRODUCE FRUIT !!!

Warren Buffet, "the Oracle of Omaha" has been buying up American stocks during this recession of 2009. His sage advice is, "Be Greedy When Others are Fearful." It's the most famous of all Buffett-isms: "Be fearful when others are greedy and greedy when others are fearful." Today there is ample evidence that people are scared and pulling money from their stock portfolios. By contrast Buffett is putting his money to work. (Money magazine, Dec. 08, Page 66)

Life will present many opportunities but it will take self-discipline, courage, and perseverance to make those opportunities a reality.

2. Courage

Paul said there was a great door of opportunity, with many adversaries.

If you think the devil lays down as you seize your opportunity you are wrong, sometimes there is opposition. Sometimes great opposition, therefore seizing your opportunity will require courage. As the children of Israel stood on the banks of the Jordon ready to inhabit the promised land the one attribute they needed more than any other was courage.

God told Joshua, "Moses is dead, now you, Joshua, and this people **get ready!**" *Joshua 1:1-2 paraphrase* That's what God is saying to us today. King David is dead, Peter and Paul have finished their race, Smith Wigglesworth and John G. Lake are

72

gone.   Demos Shakarian is no longer shaking a generation of businessmen for Jesus.

It's YOUR TURN NOW..... It's my turn now !

Slap the person next to you in the face and tell them, "It's your turn now!" Just joking.

Joshua 1:6-9 As God prepared his people to seize their opportunity three times he told them to be strong and courageous, once it is phrased be strong and very courageous !   Because God is with you ! So courage is indispensable for seizing opportunities.   And courage is not the absence of fear, it's the going forward even in the presence of fear.

During the worst part of World War 2 Winston Churchill exhorted his countrymen, "Let us brace ourselves to our duties, and so bear ourselves that if the British Commonwealth should last for a thousand years men will say, this was our finest hour !"

Our finest hour. Finest hours are not spent lying on the beach in the sun.   Finest hours are not spent on vacation, although many fine hours are, and I wish I could prosper more so that I could vacation more often. But finest hours are like when David slew Goliath and a whole NATION was emboldened by the courage of a teenager !   Finest hours are like when we recently saw 250 people born again one night in our Philippine crusade!   Finest hours are when you help your local church win a victory.

Many of us, in our walk with God, are like David at the moment he saw Bathsheba.   It was the spring, the time when kings go off to war, yet David had lost his vision and was at home lounging around the castle watchin' the babe. Vacations are great, necessary at times, hobbies are good and well. But

73

some of us used to have a real passion to do the work of God, but now we just need more and more time for vacations or hobbies. Let's not become so complacent that at the time when Kings are supposed to go to war we stay lounging around the castle.

Brace yourself to your duties !

Be strong and courageous !

Go to war and seize that opportunity !

3. Perseverance

It will take perseverance to make your opportunity a reality. I so enjoyed hearing Brian Houston preach in last years VISION conference in Seattle. He said people look at all what they're doing with Hillsong church and outreach and think it's so AMAZING. He said, ya it's GOD, but it's also TIME. It's just making a few more gains each year for 25 years. He said, "see time as your friend not as your enemy, time is a gift God has given us to bring things to pass in the earth - so build off what you've accomplished, don't always be changing visions and directions...stick with some things long enough to see a harvest."

There is a tree called the Chinese Bamboo. You must water and fertilize this tree every day for the first four years and the growth of the tree is so minimal that it looks like nothing is happening. However during the fifth year the tree grows up to ninety feet in a year ! (Ibid. Page 17 Jerry S.) Our trouble is that we want fifth year results without faithfully watering and fertilize the tree for the first four years. To see your opportunity become a reality it's going to take perseverance. EVEN through times when the going gets tough.

Charles Spurgeon said, "With great perseverance even the

snail made the ark." The other animals and even Noah were probably ready to give up on him. Can't you just see them standing on the deck, come on snail the clouds have rolled in, the rains will be starting, hurry up ! But the snail just kept pluggin' and he eventually made it. What about you ? Are you determined to persevere in what God has called you to do ? When an opportunity comes your way are you so willing to persevere that you'll crawl inch by inch if you have to, in order to make your dream a reality ? If you are you can count on the Holy Spirit to supply the power to keep you moving forward. (Ibid. Page 16)

The nose of a bulldog is slanted backward so that when it locks its jaws around something, hopefully not your leg, it can keep breathing even if it must stay clamped down for a long time. Be like that bulldog, utilize perseverance to make your dream a reality.

Persevere to make that dream a reality, persevere also to finish your spiritual course; Paul said fight the good fight, finish the race. Finish the race God has called you to run!

Some of you started the fight with great emotion and lightness of foot but you got hit a few too many times, maybe you've lowered your guard, maybe you are no longer getting up after the 8 count. Micah 7:8 says though I fall, I shall arise. Get back on your feet. God didn't call you to start this race only. HE called you to finish the race ! I feel like I've got back up more than any man alive because I was a full blown sinner before coming to Jesus and some of the thought patterns I'd developed have not let go easily. One of my nicknames was "Bud the stud" and sometimes I still catch my eyes wandering and my thoughts reverting to pre-conversion patterns. But I keep catching myself and getting my mind back on track. I get up one more time than I fall. That attitude is enabling me to finish my race. Sorry if my honesty here disappoints you but people said a guy like me could NEVER CHANGE. Many thought I was fakin' it when I started coming to church. But I've been getting up more than I fall and have been staying the course one day a time now for over 25 years. (Thanks mostly to my lovely and very attractive wife; Jaekyung.)

One last thought about opportunity; what if we step out and fail ?
Do you know how to spell faith ?   Faith is spelled R.I.S.K.. There is always a risk involved with ventures of faith. We want to be careful planners and minimize that risk if possible but any great venture will carry with it risk.

And the fear of failure holds back everyone but the champions. Michael Jordan missed more game winning shots than probably any man alive. He also made more game winning shots than anybody. While Babe Ruth was breaking the record for most home runs in a season he was also breaking the record for the most strike outs in a season. Have you failed ? All of us have, but champions don't let failure stop them. They realize failure is not final and setbacks are not permanent. They keep PLAYING UNTIL THEY WIN and so can you !

Henry Ford said, failure is just another opportunity to more intelligently start over again.   At least now you know what not to do.

When inventing the light bulb, after Edison had tried 5,000 times without success his associate asked him, how does it feel to have failed 5,000 times? He replied, "I didn't fail 5,000 times, I have identified 5,000 ways that it won't work. I am 5,000 experiments closer to finding the solution." It took him 11,000 experiments before finding the carbon impregnated filament which made the light bulb a reality. Imagine - 11,000 experiments after you'd been called a failure at 5,000. It took him 32,000 tries before he perfected the reproduction of the human voice in what he would later call the phonograph. But he didn't quit. He seized his opportunity through perseverance. (Ibid. page 52)

Don't let the fear of failure hold you back.
Every pioneer runs some risks. We pioneered Love and Faith Church and World Outreach from nothing. We had no money and no-one who wanted to join yet I told my beautiful wife Jaekyung, "look at the great opportunity before us hon we can turn our world around one person at a time and also have a vehicle which our whole congregation can drive all over the world in world outreach." She said, "sounds like a lot of work," I said, "it will be, it's an opportunity dressed in work clothes. I offer you nothing but spiritual warfare and hard work with little thanks but maybe when you and I are old sitting in our rockin' chairs we'll look back and say, *this was our finest hour* !" She said, "what if we fail?" I replied, "what if we succeed?" Her final question was, "who's gonna come?" I replied, "I was hopin' that you might come!" I then found a paralyzed guy who couldn't go anywhere and I brought my pulpit into his bedroom and preached to him on Sunday morning; Love and Faith Church was born. Don't let work, or fear of failure hold you back. You are an overcomer.

This is a stirring message and it should be. I want to just give a balance to this message about seizing the opportunity. There is a time for the christian servant of God to get down to business in the business world. Scripture says "be not slothful in business." The word says seek ye first the Kingdom of God and his righteousness and all other things shall be added unto you. It does not say seek ye **only** the Kingdom of God. As we prioritize the Kingdom of God by putting our local church, and our tithe, and God's interests first, sometimes God will use our diligence in the world of commerce, service, trade, and business to "add all things unto us."

But from time to time there may come things which look like an "opportunity" which really have to be prayed through very carefully. For instance at one point Jesus was offered "all the kingdoms of this world and the splendor thereof." If ever there was an opportunity to be seized baby there it was, talk about advance, from peasant rabbi to king of the world, that looked good ! But Jesus didn't seize it because it violated his basic priorities.

Don't allow opportunities to make more money to take you away from your place in God's plan and God's house. In many buildings pillars are essential to hold up the roof and cover the house. In the living room underneath you there are little kids playing and day by day they are growing and getting their legs under them. You are important, if you, as a pillar, are all of a sudden removed the harshness of the elements could cause great harm to the kids and the family. For some of you what looks like an opportunity may arise which would take you away from your role as a pillar in your church. Be careful and be prayerful about these "opportunities", if it's really of God it will be established over a period of time and during that period of time you should seek to multiply yourself and pray in somebody to fill your shoes so that if the time came where it was RIGHT for you to move then the house and the kids in the house won't suffer because of it. As pastor, I shouldn't forsake this flock without raising up a qualified replacement and you as a pillar should think in the same terms. The other balance to seizing the opportunity is that many times if something seems too good to be true it is. If the salesman is telling you this offer just can't wait maybe you should pass. Proverbs also says, don't be hasty and miss the way. Nevertheless genuine opportunities will come your way that must be seized.

This is such a powerful series that every time I preach it I myself go to a new level of blessing and prosperity. Partly because God confirms his word with signs following and mostly because the practical keys given in this acrostic work well in real life. I like messages that work well in real life. I've heard sermons that I got excited about, but when I tried to put the message into practice, it just didn't work. Maybe worked fine in TV land but it didn't work in real life.

This is a message that will work for you and produce a harvest if you put into practice. Don't be like the man in the book of James who used God's word like a mirror but didn't bother to comb his hair or tidy up his face. He just had a look to see what he looked like then went his own way without changing a thing. James say THE DOER of God's word will be blessed !

One of the first times I preached this acrostic after this section about seizing the opportunity I was driving in Kalispell and saw a Camaro for sale. It had been $6500.00 but was marked down to $3700.00. I thought to myself, *that is pretty cheap for a classic year Camaro.* I found it was a 1971 Super Sport worth a fair amount but it was being sold in midwinter for a song. I thought surely I must seize this opportunity. God, wife, and friends helped me find money, which I didn't think I had, and I rushed back down there. I was dickering with the guy about the car but found his price was firm. Just then a turbocharged GMC Denali drove up and 5 teenagers piled out and hurried toward us. I grabbed my $3700. cash and handed it to the guy saying, "I'll take the car." The teens had $3700. in their hand and said, "here's your money sir we want the car." He replied, "sorry this guy bought it about 2 seconds ago." Opportunities don't always wait for the timid or the slow to act, many times they must be seized. I put a $3,000.00 paint job on the car and within a year it was worth about twice what I had into it. Many have wanted to buy it from me but it remains my Sunday go to meeting car in the summer. I preach real good after kicking in the four barrels and hearing the dual exhaust roar on my way to church. (And God is delighting in the prosperity of his servant.)

The last time I preached this series I felt convicted because we had possessed, by seizing the opportunity, highway frontage property that had great potential but we had never built the type of business that would capitalize on that potential. I told, earlier in the book, how we went forth with the new building but it was preaching this message that inspired me to do it. After preaching this series again I was getting some counsel from some of our church leaders about me stepping out and building and Virginia said, "just put into practice what you just preached and seize the opportunity." So I practiced what I preached and so we have prospered.

Get this teaching into your mind and spirit. Act upon it wisely and you will reap the reward of seizing your opportunity. At the age of eighty-three the great architect Frank Lloyd Wright was asked, "Which of the beautiful structures you've designed and built do you consider your greatest masterpiece?" He answered, "my next one." Which is your greatest opportunity ? It could be "your next one." (Ibid., page 79) While we are still on O I'm going to address another O word that is vital;

⑩.rganize   Chapter 8

Organize - Give structure, arrange, put into working order.

When you begin to go through the steps we've discussed, plan, rid of poverty mentality, seize opportunity; there will probably be more for you to manage, to oversee, to keep track of.

And if right now you can't even keep track of your check book, your cell phone, or your bank balance. How in the world are you going to keep your act together if increase comes your direction?

The prophet Jeremiah asks, "If you have raced with men on foot and they have worn you out, how can you compete with horses ? If you stumble in safe country how will you manage in the thickets by the Jordan?"   Jeremiah 12:5

That means if you can't keep your kitchen clean you could never have a restaurant. If you can't balance your household finances it would be very difficult to run your own business. But if we just got organized so many of us would be positioned for increase.

What is organize ? It means to Give structure, arrange, put in working order.   I run a large business, have rentals and 15 storage units, oversee a church, and deal with a world outreach ministry.   But I've got a track to run on because I've thrown away the worthless little check book ledgers and utilize a nice accounting book for each enterprise and that simple act of organization keeps things going smoothly if I don't get behind. (My daughter helps manage the storage units.)

The Kingdom of God is all about faithfulness and increase, remember the parable ? Faithful over little, ruler over much. God tells the one guy, you've been faithful to pastor 5 people therefore now take charge of 5 cities. And it's going to take a higher degree of organization to administrate 5 cities.

Josiah said to his friend, "how come you're not married?, Here you are 19 years old and you don't have a wife." Chris responded, "I can't even take care of my own life how do you think I can take care of a wife too." Jo replied, "that's what you get a wife for.... so they can take care of YOU!" That's a real hopeful theory but it would be a whole lot better if the guy could get his own act together and then get married.

My wife really wanted a new car or at least a relatively new car. She didn't know it but I was down at the dealership 2 Christmas's ago thinking of getting her one. But I went for a ride in the car she was using and after seeing what a mess it was in I told her, "you're not ready for a new car you can't even keep an old car clean and take care of it." She didn't like my conclusion but the very next day she was listening to Gloria Copeland preach and as she was teaching Gloria said, "some people want a new car but will not get it because they are not even taking good care of the one they have." After that she reluctantly agreed she wasn't ready and we bought her an old ugly $2,000. Camry. She was diligent keeping that cheap car clean, organized, and washed - then one year later we got her a brand new 2008 Camry. God's hand is not shortened that he cannot bless and promote us but first we must get organized and faithful with what we already have !

God in these days is calling us to be super*natural* people *super*natural people not **super wierd !**

There are some SUPER things we need in this hour; things like faith, things like God's burden removing, yoke destroying anointing, things like the favor of God which opens doors no man can shut.

But in addition to these SUPER things, there are a lot of natural things we need to get in order. Things we need to do in the NATURAL, in order to cooperate with the SUPER! One of these things is to ORGANIZE.

If God dumped his super on some Christian's lives all that would result is SUPER CHAOS.

Because their natural lives are out of order.

We need to get our lives in ORDER.

There is something about order that is respected by heaven!

There is something about getting our family in order,
  our marriage in order,
        our finances in order,
              our garage in order,
                    our living situation in order,
                          THAT IS RESPECTED BY HEAVEN.

There is power and anointing released through organization even in the natural. A lot of us want to dump the responsibility for us to prosper on God,
        without doing what we can do.
but the Holy Spirit is not an initiator HE IS A HELPER.
        He comes alongside to help us as we take the initiative.

Some of you want God to help you get out of debt, but if you don't take action, He can't help you. You should be able to tell God right down to the penny exactly how much you need to pay off your debts, write it down, make it plain on tablets, then watch the power of God month by month, week by week, and day by day, make you into the head and not the tail! Jesus said speak to the mountain and don't doubt in your heart and it must be removed. But if you haven't even taken time to carefully itemize and prioritize your debts and **declare a war upon** them then you have not even defined the mountain you intend to speak to.

It's the small foxes that spoil the vine, it's not always the big things. Organization can open you up for the "and suddenly's." Organization can set you up for the miracle working power of God to invade your affairs.

Do you remember Jesus in Matthew 14 and John 6 when he is getting ready to feed 5,000 people with five loaves and two fish? He said sit the people down in groups of 50 and groups of 100. This shows me he's concerned about order and organization . He broke the bread and began the miracle only *after* ORDER had been established.

If you want God to inject his SUPER into your natural then you better get your natural in order. Because God is a God of order, and we must come to the place where we judge what's out of order in our life. We must come to the place where we judge what's out of order in our marriage,
       what's out of order in our business,
          what's out of order in our relationships,
             what's out of order in our surfing of the net.
Before God shows up there has to be order.
We can't have Jezebel running the show with Ahab laying on the couch watching TV.

We have to get things in order or we're holding back the power of God!

84

It's time for the church to get in order,
   to get rid of the fornication,
      to get rid of the strife and envy,
         to get rid of the disobedience,
            and position our lives for blessing.

Why ? Because we are expecting the miraculous to invade the church, and it's not going to happen till we get things in order!

A court of law does not proceed until they establish order. When the Judge sees disorder, he brings his gavel down and says ORDER IN THE COURT !
I believe God is sayin' ORDER IN THE HOUSE !   There is a whole movement in America where people have forsaken "organized religion" in favor of disorganized religion. They have opted for a church or fellowship situation which is just basically a few families gathering together in a home "edifying" each other with no real leader. Any attempt at "gathering in his name" is better than nothing but that scenario will never equal the blessing of being in a God ordained, New Testament, apostolic church under clear lines of government and apostolic fathering. (In our church "I am a man under authority, *and I can tell you exactly who they are*, with people under me." and the blessing of the fathers flows to the children.)

In Malachi 3:7 God says "Even from the days of my fathers you have turned aside from my ordinances, *ordinance is another word for order*, return to me and I will return to you says the Lord of Hosts." In other words get in order and I'll return to you...get your mouth, thought life, giving, church life in order and the miraculous will be restored to you.

Divine order is a prerequisite for miracles, when we get organized, we set ourself up for the "and suddenly's" which God is well able to do. Here's a great example from God's word; 2 Chronicles chapter 29;

In this chapter Hezekiah is beginning to reign.

In verse 3 in the first month of his first year, (seek ye first the kingdom) he is opening the doors of the temple and repairing them.

In verse 5 he is sanctifying the priests and commanding them to get the filthiness out of God's house.

In verse 10 Hezekiah is making a covenant of obedience to restore temple order and worship.

In verse 17 to 20 the priests are cleansing the temple and sanctifying the vessels.

In verse 21 Hezekiah is offering a holy offering in sets of sevens.

In verse 25 the worship team is set in place according to the commandment of the apostolic father, David.

In verse 31 to 34 abundant burnt offerings are being presented.

Then verse 35 and 36 summarizes the events; So the service in the house of the Lord **was set in order.** And Hezekiah **rejoiced**, and **all the people rejoiced** over what *God had prepared* for the people, **for the thing was done SUDDENLY.**

Friends when you get things SET IN ORDER, and organized, then you can rejoice, the people with you will rejoice, and God will begin to do some "and suddenly's" in your life and situation.

And suddenly, they got out of debt.

And suddenly, their kid's got saved.

And suddenly, the miracle working power of God began to flow into their situation because they got it set in order - then heaven saw and respected that order, and God accomplished something in a short time that man couldn't accomplish in a long time because ORGANIZATION gave the freight train of the Holy Spirit a track to run on !

(Much of the material for this chapter on organize came from a preaching tape by Dr. Creflo Dollar of World Changers Church International in Atlanta. Strategies for Debt Removal; Organize)

Application;

* Declare war on your debts then itemize them in terms of priority. Make it clear on a page in your computer which debts are due first, which ones are higher in priority because of a higher interest rate, and what is the total amount you owe. Keep this page updated and share it regularly with your spouse if you have one. It's amazing how this will bring unity to your financial vision. Keep old copies of your "War on Debt" in your computer so you can occasionally see how far you've progressed. How do you expect God to deliver you from debt if you are not organized enough to tell God exactly what your debts are ?

* Clean and organize your desk, office, garage, car, and jockey box.

* Go through your computer and delete files that are no longer relevant. Your computer will run faster.

If you have faith as a grain of mustard seed, ye shall say unto this mountain, remove hence to yonder place; and it shall remove; and nothing shall be impossible unto you. MT.17:20

The modern day pioneer of "seed-faith" giving would have to be Oral Roberts. In a nutshell he describes the revelation God gave him;   Jesus incredible teaching on the seed and wrapping our faith around it opened my eyes wide;
Faith has to be like a seed, even if it's only a small seed. A seed is something you sow to reap a harvest, to receive a return. When that seed is sown as our act of faith, it opens the way for us to speak to our mountain of need and command it to be removed.   I saw that Christianity is not a system of diminishing return but it is a multiplication of the more abundant life.

God showed him there were 3 principles of seed faith giving;
1. Make God your source.
2. Sow your seed as an act of your faith in God.
3. Expect a miracle harvest to follow in due season.

Oral received harsh persecution for bringing these truths to the public eye but others, rather than persecuting him, practiced the path in the word he had pioneered and have seen miracle harvests. Dr. Creflo Dollar believes in this concept so much that he says, "there is no need that a seed will not meet."   When he was building the faith dome in Atlanta the project needed several million to continue but all they had was $770,000. He went before God about the need and God told him, "You don't have enough for the need but you do have enough for a seed." Creflo told the board they were to give all they had to another church with a building program. They gave it all and shortly thereafter their own need was abundantly supplied.

God kind of tricked me into seed faith giving. I was against the "faith message" in general and many of the teachers I'm quoting in this work turned me off at one stage. Then God spoke to me clearly during a 7-8 day fast to do some major giving. My heroes were missionaries and I felt the reason God wanted me to give was so that I could become "poor like Jesus" and live the rest of my life helping the poor like Mother Theresa. Soon we found ourselves helping street kids and pioneering a church in a squalid ghetto in Jamaica. We were obeying the word God had spoken to me during the fast.

In retrospect our ministry in Jamaica was primarily a season of sowing seed. At times we ourselves were dirt poor but we were sowing major seed. We truly enjoyed seeing people helped but there was an aspect of this season, mainly struggling ourselves, that was no fun. Scripture speaks of the sowing end of the equation in terms that are not all that glowing; *Those who sow in tears will reap with songs of joy. He who goes out weeping, carrying seed to sow, will return with songs of joy carrying sheaves with him.* Psalm 126:5-6

At the time I thought I was just fulfilling my destiny as a champion of the poor but God began taking me through the steps Oral Roberts mentioned. First God spoke to me very clearly that I was to repent for ever trusting anything or anybody as the source of my supply and that from that moment on I was to look to him as my source. (His emphasis in this was my heart, he was not saying to me that I should never share a need...the body of Christ is a unit and even in a natural body there is communication between various parts via the nerve paths and the central computer; brain) I repented and began to look to God Almighty as my ultimate source.

Next God put me in a position where I had to hear the word of faith. Though at this time I did not esteem "the faith message" I had grown to greatly esteem word of faith missionaries in Africa and now in Jamaica. While other missionaries were wincing under the powers of darkness these faith cats were pioneering powerful churches and shouting the victory. I had previously stereotyped "the faith message" as a bunch of slick dudes who were claiming Cadillacs but as I looked deeper I found powerful ambassadors of God who were living to give and to be a blessing.

I was on a board for helping Montego Bay's street people with several great "Faith" pastors and they kept emphasizing to me how God would return back to us the seed we were sowing "good measure, pressed down, and running over in due season." The hundredfold return was also being taught to us.

At this time I was preaching in Love and Faith World Outreach in Kingston Jamaica and when I was done an old prophetess from the congregation told me, "as you were preaching my bible was open to a certain verse and I saw your face in that verse." What verse ?, I asked, Mark 11:24 she replied; "Therefore I tell you, whatever you ask for in prayer, believe that you have received it and you shall have it." As I meditated on that verse later I thought, "woa baby where have you been all my life ?, I could have used you when we were unable to afford our rent, I could use you right now as we desperately need a vehicle." God led me to believe I received some things; On the top of the list was 300 souls (conversions), I believed for a quality air-conditioned vehicle, a nice

90

four bedroom house to own, and other things. Everything on the list is now fulfilled and more. I thought it would all happen in Jamaica but God moved us from Jamaica to newly opened Russia for three months to fulfill the majority of the 300 conversions and moved us to Montana to fulfill other items on the list.

When God first taught me these truths about sowing He went way out of his way to illustrate his point because I was a sceptic. At this time we were missionaries in Jamaica on a weekly food budget of $25.00 in a country where food is twice as expensive as in the U.S.A.. Every week we could afford only one chicken and that was the edible highlight of my week. I came home one day and Jaekyung told me she had given away our weekly chicken ! I was teed off but tried to keep from exploding. Before week's end someone came by and out of the blue gave us a tremendous chicken that was way bigger than the one my wife had sowed !

If your seeds don't sprout overnight don't discard this truth, because many seeds take time to grow, but God kept doing the insta-seed harvest with me just to show me it was for real. Next I went to a mountain lake with a buddy to fish. I caught a small trout. I told God, "this will not meet my need for a good dinner so I'll use it as a seed," I released it. I caught a nine inch rainbow next and said, "God that worked so well I think I'll sow this one in faith also." Next I landed a good sized fish and proceeded to reel in trout after succulent trout. Meanwhile my friend, who was using the same bait, hadn't caught a thing all afternoon so the next fish I caught I exclaimed, "Dale I'm sowing this fish in faith for YOU to receive a harvest." Straightway he caught the biggest fish of the day !

I became a believer of "seed-faith giving." More recently we've pioneered a church through "seed-faith" principles. Starting a church from nothing is an adventure...when no-one is asking you to start a church, or wanting to come, where do you begin? I knew a man who was bedfast so I decided to bring my pulpit to his living room in Evergreen and preach to him. That morning his wife decided to also stay for the service. The next week I believed God for six to seven people and a $200.00 offering. This couple had once had a gargantuan great-dane named Goliath. As I arrived that morning for service the first thing I saw was this giant dog house with "Goliath" painted on it. I felt like Goliath was calling my name telling me nothing would come of this insignificant beginning but as I quietly held on to my faith six to seven people **did arrive** for service in the well worn living-room. My heart sank however when I noticed that the offering was miniscule, just a few crinkled up ones. Instead of taking my faith off the job by verbalizing defeat I kept my mouth shut about it and just kept visiting the congregation. As a trucker was leaving he said, "good service pastor we'll see you next week." Then he stopped before going out the door, pulled out his wallet, peeled off two one hundred dollar bills and walked back into the living room and put them in the offering hat !

Next I believed that we as a congregation would never rent but would own. I'd just looked at a lovely five acre parcel on the highway with a run down shop building on it which I saw had potential. That night I woke up and walked out to the kitchen. The oven clock read 3:33 and the Holy Spirit nudged me, call unto me and I'll show you great and mighty things you know not of. (Jeremiah 33:3) I got down to business and said, "OK God I'm calling right now, are you talking to me about that land I saw today ? I opened my Bible and it said, ask and it will be given..... I replied "you are talking to me about it aren't you ?" I turned the Bible to a different spot and it was the identical text in a different gospel. (I don't normally play Bible roulette like that but God used it that night.)

From that moment I had faith but almost no money. Only enough money for a seed. So I sowed to other churches that needed a permanent home. Particularly to a first nations congregation in Browning, Montana. Meanwhile we made an offer on the land and they accepted it. But in the offer I told them we'd give them 10 grand at closing and we didn't even have $200.00 left after putting $500.00 earnest money down. The closing was scheduled for right after Easter Sunday. God had healed a man through the ministry and he put in several thousand at the Easter Sunday service. Others also helped and when the day came we had the money !

Maybe you are like we were, you don't have enough money to meet your need but you do have enough for a seed. Last week I noticed a leader of our church stepped out in faith and did some giving. I happen to know things were tight for them so I complimented him on the giving. Within four days he received a four thousand dollar unexpected bonus from work then his landlord came by and said he'd forgot to cash one of their rent checks so he was just going to give it back and not require them to write another ! A Miracle harvest during the mid-winter 2009 recession. Let's continue examining this principle;

Sowing

As long as the earth remains seedtime and harvest, cold and heat, summer and winter, day and night will never cease -Genesis 8:22

God has placed certain laws in the earth which will never change. So since these laws will never change or adapt to us we should adapt to them. In Montana the cold and heat, summer and winter, law is very noticeable. Even though I was born and raised here I've never found a way to change that law. There are ways however to adapt to it so that the cold winter is more enjoyable; such as getting a ski pass or doing cross country ski racing- which I enjoy.

Another law that we cannot change but can adapt to is seed-time and harvest. Our life is like a seed, our time is like a seed, our words are like seeds, and our money can become like a seed, and the seed can turn into a harvest. But in order for it to do so we must learn and put into practice the laws and principles which govern seedtime and harvest, or what some passages refer to as sowing and reaping.

Even before I was a Christian we'd talk about how you reap what you sow, or how bad Karma was coming upon us. But we never stopped to think about who kept track of the Karma. You do reap what you sow, God keeps track of what you sow, and the Bible talks about sowing and reaping financially. The Bible pictures you and your money like a farmer and his crop. That farmer may want nothing more than to eat every last kernel of corn, but he can't do it. The laws of seedtime and harvest dictate he'd better plant some of that crop back into the soil so he has a harvest next year. If he's smart he will take THE BEST of his seed and replant it. If he wants a big harvest he'll plant as much seed back as he can.

So often Christian people are like a farmer who **really doesn't believe that seed will multiply** and produce a harvest so they just consume all the crop...*you never know what tomorrow's gonna bring so you might as well just eat it while you have it,* is the mentality. They have a great feast for awhile but when it's all gone, you ask, HEY BRO how's it goin ? "Not so good", they reply "but **I'm just waiting for my ship to come in."** The problem however **is that they never sent a ship out to begin with**, so according to the laws of sowing and reaping, God is going to return unto them exactly what they sowed, nothing. You can wait a long time for your ship to come in If you never sent one out. Because you can not lay claim to promises you do not qualify for. Did you receive your year end dividend from Bill Gates and Microsoft ? Did you get yours ? The reason you didn't get any is that you did not invest in Microsoft. That's the same reason many people don't receive much from the hand of God.... they fail to INVEST IN HIS ENTERPRISE, in his company, in his kingdom.. ON the other hand when you begin to give into God's kingdom, you are storing your treasure up above where neither moth nor rust eats it up and then, WHEN YOU HAVE A NEED, God meets your need *according to His riches in GLORY.* YOU GET A DIVIDEND and a withdrawal from your heavenly bank account.

One man gives freely, yet gains even more;
another **withholds unduly, but comes to poverty.**
A generous man will prosper;
he who refreshes others will himself be refreshed. Prov. 11:24-25

Consider **2 Corinthians 9** vs.1 Now about ministering to the saints KJV. The Amplified version of the Bible translates that; *NOW about the offering.*

Here Paul is talking to the Corinthians about the offering; it's biblical for the preacher to talk to the people about the offering. We don't need to just put a box in the foyer and think we're spiritual because we never talk about the offering.

Here Paul is taking two chapters to talk about the offering before he receives it; Verse 5; Not as an extortion, wrung out of you, but as a generous and willing gift. The point of this verse is Paul saying, don't let something as important as your sowing be dictated or determined BY NEED or by emotional manipulation and hyped up promises. But Paul says think about your giving in advance, PLAN how you can be generous this week or this month, or this year.

If you don't PLAN your giving then what happens is you give God the leftovers. You just cruise through your year and do your giving to either the CAUSE THAT WHINES THE LOUDEST. Or the hype you can't resist.....*according to the Jewish calendar if you give to my ministry TODAY you will receive a seven fold restoration of all you've ever lost.* You wait for the whine or the hype and then give your leftovers. Rather than really planning with aforethought the amounts you will sow and deciding carefully what good ground you will sow INTO.

He goes on; each man should give what he has decided in his heart to give. Paul is saying plan your sowing and determine how much you can give without getting a poor me attitude. BUT AS YOU SET THE AMOUNT, REMEMBER vs. 6 says; Whoever sows sparingly will also reap sparingly, and whoever sows generously will also reap generously. Paul is teaching that in the law of seedtime and harvest YOU determine the size of the harvest. Jesus confirmed that in *Luke 6:38 Give and it shall be given back unto you. A good measure, pressed down, shaken together, and running over, will be poured into your lap. For with the measure you use, it will be measured back to you.*

The Amplified says, for with the measure you use when you confer benefits on others, it will be measured back to you.

Both verses here talk about MEASURE. You determine

whether you use a teaspoon, a shovel, a dump truck load, or a supertanker. Then when you pray the prayer of Jabez, "Oh God that you would bless me indeed." God says, "OK give me the measure which you predetermined; teaspoon, shovel, or dump truck, or supertanker." So in harvest cycle, God uses that measure to give back to you.

Now don't get under condemnation if you have to start small. Start with what you have, not with what you don't have. Some of us had to start with a miniature measure and work up. I heard of a guy who had no money, but really wanted to give, but the only thing he had was zucchinis. He began hilariously dispensing zucchinis from his garden. Pretty soon everyone at church would lock their car before going into the service so they wouldn't come back to a seat full of zucchinis ! My daughter wouldn't have locked her car. She's the only person I know who loves zucchinis.

In view of the truth that you determine the measure Paul said in verse 7, *LET EACH GIVE AS HE HAS DECIDED in his heart for God loves a cheerful giver.* We hear that a lot, God loves a cheerful giver. But part of what makes a person cheerful according to the verse is that they are giving what they have decided in their own heart to give. Not sorrowfully or because the preacher is making them feel guilty. Paul's teaching here is talking about the offering not about tithing. Tithing is the biblical concept that 10% of our income belongs to God for the work of the local church. You don't set **that** measure, God already set it, he said 10 %. (Some tightwads have a problem with tithing, I never did because I spent way more than 10% on drugs and suds before coming to Christ so to give 10% to the savior who gave his life to change mine, for his favorite project the church, to me is a small thing for God to ask.) Offerings however are gifts you decide to give which most people consider should be over and above the tithe; gifts to the poor, to special speakers, to missions... I'm sure the principles Paul talks about here also apply to tithers. I'm sure GOD loves a cheerful tither, rather than a mad tither. But the pastor doesn't care if you're cheerful or mad he's just happy you did it.   God, on the other hand, treats the cheerful giver with V.I.P. treatment; for God loves, that is he takes pleasure in, prizes above other things, and is unwilling to abandon or do without a cheerful prompt to do it giver whose heart is in the giving. (vs. 7 Amplified version.)

I don't sing those phony songs like "JESUS you're all I WANT." He's not all I want; He's my number one desire - I seek first the kingdom - but there's other things I want.... Sometimes I want some popcorn, a new guitar, mags for my truck. Sometimes I want Jaekyung to quit makin' kimchee and come to bed; Jesus doesn't meet my every need you know ! Part of me is just a dude that wants things. Because of that there's a part of me that would only cheerfully give very little. *"OK then, if God only wants me to give what I can happily give then I'll just give a quarter. Because I'd really rather get a ski pass, go to Hawaii, or use the money for eating out."*

For those of you realists like me, who have other things you might like to use the money for, sometimes we need to challenge ourselves in the area of sowing. Yes God loves a cheerful giver, but the other side of the story is that if we don't challenge ourselves to plant some significant seeds today, we will not have a significant harvest tomorrow !

Some of the giving we've done that has really moved the heart of God, and has triggered mega returns, hasn't been done in a real smiley way. Yes, we loved God, yes, we were excited to help people, but some of our biggest giving has been out of sheer determination to obey the word of God. No goose bumps, no holy laughter, just obedience. He that sows in tears, will reap with shouts of JOY !

The farmer may not be that turned on about planting the best of his crop back into the dirt, but when he does the right thing, he will one day REAP with shouts of joy!

On occasion Jesus challenged people to go beyond "cheerful giving" into what would have made them extremely blessed. One day a handsome young man with a nicely oiled face and Gucci jeans dismounted his camel drawn carriage and ran up to Jesus saying, "good master what must I do to inherit the kingdom." Jesus was still in the process of building his apostolic team and saw in this young heart an enthusiasm that would fit right in with Peter and the gang. He told him, "if you really want to go all the way son, sell everything you have and give it to the poor." This was a challenge to go way beyond "cheerful giving." This was a unique invitation into the world of the miraculous. The invitation was refused and the young man walked away sad. From then on, the riches he'd accumulated never really excited him the way they once had. From then on, every time he climbed into a new chariot, he wondered, "what if I had obeyed him?"

Peter, who had watched the encounter at at distance said, "Master, at the same fork in the road, we did give up our goods and follow you. What will happen to us ?" Jesus replied, I tell you the truth, no one who has left houses or brothers or sisters or mother or father or children or lands for me and the gospel will fail to receive a hundred times as much in this present age (houses, brothers, sisters, mothers, children and fields---and with them persecutions) and in the age to come eternal life. Mark 10:29 Jesus told Peter that the rich young man forfeited a 100 fold multiplication of everything he would have given up. He missed the greatest financial opportunity of his life not to mention the joy of apostleship. I know a modern day rich young ruler who obeyed the exact same instruction when the Lord spoke to him. This individual gave up lands, a house, and vehicles to the poor and followed Jesus. Some years later, I've noticed he has received numerous lands, houses, vehicles, and now they take in, in ONE YEAR's time, the large amount they had originally given to the poor when they abandoned all for the gospel.

This is not science fiction, Jesus said, I TELL YOU THE TRUTH, I will multiply back unto you the houses, lands and people you've given up for my gospel 100 fold in this present age. Not in heaven, in this age, in this time, IN THIS LIFE-TIME. Say, *"in this lifetime."* Sowing doesn't always produce instant results. In Ecclesiastes Solomon said cast your bread upon the waters, give portions to seven even to eight, for you don't know what disaster may come upon the land. I believe the tithe goes to the local church but in our offering it's not a bad idea to distribute the offering in several places, portions to seven even to eight. This, according to Solomon, is great recession insurance because when you have given he later says "and after many days" it will come back to you on every wave. How long is "many days"? A minute? An hour? A week? No, many days is many days.

Jesus promised the hundredfold return would work not immediately but continuously throughout the rest of your lifetime. I believe that through faith you can make withdrawals from your heavenly bank account and expedite the return but this is not an instant lottery type proposition. It's a heavenly invest-ment that pays dividends throughout your lifetime...with per-secutions. (God delights in the prosperity of his servant but the devil does not, the reaping we've done has been done right in the presence of our enemy with him resisting us at every

100

curve. There are also jealous people who will arise, and other Christians, who do not delight in the prosperity of God' servant, and they will persecute you. Especially if you pastor a church - Be **nice** to your pastor !)

Jesus did not make this all or nothing offer to everyone. I believe Jesus was inviting the enthusiastic young ruler to join his apostolic team. He was offering him treasures in heaven, and a 100 fold return on the earth. He was trying to get him to let loose of the little dab that he had so that he could bring him into the laws of seedtime and harvest. But when Jesus offer went beyond "cheerful giving" the fledgling apostle went away sad.   Creflo Dollar once made the commitment that he'd give what God told him to in each offering. One day the Spirit of God told him to give $10,000.00. His first reaction was, "I rebuke you Satan."   Then he realized the devil would not tell him to give big into the work of God. He obeyed God and has seen that seed multiplied back to him many times over.

1. Sowing works on the principle of multiplication HERE and HEREAFTER.

Many people work hard, save every dime, and through ADDITION increase some until they die and go to hell. But in sowing God is offering us a life that makes a difference! Multiplication in the *here* and now, *and the hereafter.* 100 times as much is multiplication not addition. He didn't tell Peter, "you gave so I'll double your money." He said he'd multiply what Peter had given a hundredfold both in this life and in the celestial city to come.

Giving into the kingdom is God's way to take that little dab that you presently have, meet others needs with it, then multply it into a huge amount that is many times larger than what was originally sown. The little boy gave 5 loaves and 2 fish, his entire lunch, to Jesus who was able to multiply it so that it fed a multitude with 12 baskets left over. If Jesus could do that for a young boy with a lunch just think what he could have done with a rich young ruler's fortune ?!

There was a famine in the land and instead of going to Egypt, as usual, God's spirit instructed Isaac to dwell in Philistine territory. Then Isaac sowed in the land (*planted crops* NIV *sowed seed* Amplified) and received in the same year an hundredfold.(*a hundred times as much as he planted*-Amplified) The man became rich and his wealth continued to grow until he became very wealthy. Genesis 26:12-13 Here is another story of God delighting in the prosperity of his servant; The man became rich and his wealth continued to grow. But why did his wealth grow ? The answer is found in verse 12, ISSAC PLANTED CROPS, Isaac sowed seed even in a year of famine. When finances become really tight for us it's tempting to eat our seed but Isaac planted even in a year of famine.

Isaac knew this principle of sowing and reaping because he was a farmer. I've heard teachers come against what I'm teaching now and say *you should never give to get*. A farmer would think that kind of talk is plain foolishness, a farmer would think, "why in the world am I planting this valuable seed if I don't hold an expectation in my heart for a harvest ?" It's true we should give to bless and not just be thinking of what's in it for us but God wants some of you to begin to think like farmers who sow good seed in good ground and reap a multiplied harvest **so that you can become even more generous.** I've read of people who became like professional farmers where sowing is concerned.

Once Kenneth Copeland and Jerry Savelle flew to Birmingham, Alabama in Ken's little Cessna 310 to preach. While there, Ken sought God for two days about needing a bigger airplane for the ministry and about starting a TV show. Finally Kenneth had the answer, "Jerry" he said, "God showed me to plant my best seed, which is my airplane, for the harvest I need." Jerry thought, great, how are we going to get home to Fort Worth? Ken said, I'm not giving it away just yet first we'll fly it back home and I'll have the engines redone. Jerry thought, why redo the engines if you are giving it away? Ken said, "Jerry, I know what you are thinking but the seed I sow will come back to me a hundredfold. I want a bigger plane in first class condition not with engines that need redone." They flew to Fort Worth and Kenneth spent $10,000 having the engines redone. (Like $100,000 today) then gave it to a preacher who was believing God for an airplane. Eleven days later Ken called Jerry and said, "if you want to see a miracle get down here to the airport." He came and Ken said, "look down the runway". As Jerry looked the most beautiful airplane he'd seen up till that time, a Cessna 414, landed. The man got out of it, walked up to Brother Copeland, handed him the keys and said, "Here's your airplane." Eleven days after he sowed that seed, he received a bigger, faster airplane completely paid for! (Footsteps of a Prophet, Jerry Savelle, page 177)

If you are just a giver you can give worn out junk, seconds, and leftovers to God's projects but when you become a sower you pay attention to the quality of the seed you put into the ground. Note; Jerry goes on to mention that some have tried to do what Ken did, by giving away their car for instance, and have got into trouble. Jerry emphasizes that you don't give your car away because he gave his away. You give because it's a revelation to you, and because you are inspired by the Holy Ghost.

When you become a sower you also pay attention to the quality of the ground you sow into because;
2. *The size of your harvest depends on the measure you use and the fertility of the soil you sow into.*

In the parable of the sower some soil produced nothing, some thirtyfold, some sixtyfold, and some one hundredfold. In context, it's speaking of hearts receiving the gospel, but there is truth to be gleaned here for the sower as well. The fertility of the soil you sow into will be a determining factor in the harvest you receive.

Here are examples of good ground;

* The local church. Sow into what Jesus is involved with, building the church. The book of Acts is not a story of evangelism it's a story of church planting and development.

* Wise giving to the needy is also good ground.
"He who gives to the poor, lends to the Lord and God will repay him again" Pr.19:17

* Missions is productive ground which is often overlooked because of the "out of sight out of mind principle."

* Faithful, Anointed Ambassadors of God. The Philippians sowed to Paul's ministry and Paul promised them that **HIS God would supply their need** from his riches in glory. The widow sowed to the prophet and the oil flowed till her debt was paid.

3. An expectation for harvest is essential

Some people give but are so beaten down in their faith that it seems they really never reap a harvest. Expectation is an important ingredient in receiving from God. When the cripple had asked Peter and John for money Peter told him, "Look at us!" So the man gave them his attention, **expecting to receive** something from them. Acts 3:4-5

After we sow we must give God our attention, expecting to receive something. Expectation is so key. Last year I took a young guy, who'd just served a decade or so as a Navy Seal, Elk hunting with me. Elk hunting can be a lot of looking and very little finding. For a couple days we walked through the forest with outstretched ears straining to hear, but we never heard a bull respond to my bugle. Our faith was fatigued, but that night I listened to Dr. Dollar teaching about expectation, and God's word raised my expectation level.

The next day Jeremy and I hiked to the rocky summit of a big mountain, and then we laid in the sun to rest. Again all morning we heard no response. He said, "if only I could just hear one respond to a bugle it would make my day." I replied, "YOU WILL!" See the word produced an expectancy in me. I let out a good bugle and this time a bull's shrill and haunting response resounded through the valley. We worked our way down the mountain toward the hot bull and ended up bringing him in to within fifteen feet of us, but we could not quite get the right angle for a shot. (In archery hunters must be ethical in terms of shot placement) That afternoon we had two others come in to us, but it all started with an expectation. An expectation of harvest is essential.

Let's finish with the scripture we began with; 2 Corinthians 9: 6-12.

Remember this: whoever sows sparingly will also reap sparingly, and whoever sows generously will also reap generously. Let each person give as he has made up his mind and purposed in his heart, not reluctantly, sorrowfully, or under compulsion, for God loves (He takes pleasure in, prizes above other things, and is unwilling to abandon or to do without, a cheerful (joyous, prompt to do it) giver whose heart is in his giving.

And God is able to make all grace (every favor and earthly blessing) come to you in abundance, so that you may always and under all circumstances and whatever the need, be self sufficient (possessing enough to require no aid or support and furnished in abundance for every good work and charitable donation).

And God who provides seed for the sower and bread for eating will also provide and multiply your resources for sowing and increase the fruits of your righteousness (which manifests itself in active goodness, kindness and charity.)

Thus you will be enriched in all things and in every way so that you can be generous, and your generosity which is administered by us, will bring forth thanksgiving to God.

This service that you perform is not only supplying the needs of God's people but is is also overflowing in many expressions of thanks to God.

Paul ends that text by saying **your generosity will supply needs and provoke overflowing thanksgiving to God**. Once I was all dressed in white while shopping in a local supermarket. I noticed an old woman with worn out hands, wearing worn out clothes, trying to find some bargains. I took out a large bill from my wallet and walked up to her and said, "the Lord wants you to have this." As she received the bill she looked at me in shock and said, "you must be an angel !" As I saw the amazed look on her face and the tears welling up in her eyes, I couldn't resist - I just smiled and walked off - leaving her to thank God and wonder. That my friends is the life of a sower, it's a joyous and abundant life. A life where our generosity supplies needs and provokes thanksgiving to God.

Review;

A. Make God your source.
B. Sow your seed as an act of your faith in God.
C. Expect a miracle harvest to follow in due season.

1. Sowing works on the principle of multiplication *here* and *hereafter*.

2. The size of your harvest depends on the measure you use, and the fertility of the soil you sow into.

3. An expectation of harvest is essential.

℘.erseverance   Chapter 10

Acts 14:19 Some Jews came from Antioch and Iconium and won the crowd over. They stoned Paul and dragged him outside the city, thinking that he was dead. But after the disciples had gathered around him, he got up and went back into the city.

In Lystra, Paul was preaching, and as he preached, a crippled man studied him carefully and faith rose in his heart. Then Paul saw that he had faith to be healed and said, stand up on your feet ! The man jumped up and began to walk. Acts 14:8 Tradition has come up with views that Paul's thorn in the flesh was sickness or an eye disease that produced pus around the eyes. I find it hard to believe that the cripple gathered faith to be healed by studying a sick man. Paul's thorn was a messenger of Satan not a sickness ! God doesn't want you to be sick ! The cripple was watching a man of faith who had walked hundreds of miles and could still preach. A man of faith who shook off snakes from his arm. A man of faith whose preaching of a risen Christ was reflected in the preacher's vigor. It was beholding the man of faith that ignited faith in the cripple and he went walking and leaping and PRAISING GOD !

The healing of the cripple gained Paul instant fame insomuch that they thought he was a god and were going to offer sacrifices. A few verses later the crowd was persuaded to take up boulders and stone him to death. As people of God sometimes we are enshrined, other times we are scorned, but we must stay steady to our course because popularity, or the lack thereof, is a shifting sand that can change as quickly as the weather.

Earlier in our series we talked about seizing the opportunity based on Paul saying a great door of opportunity had opened unto him. The verse continued with Paul saying his opportunity was accompanied by many adversaries. Opportunities are not without challenge, in Lystra the challenge for Paul was enormous; the crowd threw huge rocks at him till all present thought he was dead. So they dragged him outside the city, possibly to the garbage dump.

This is where perseverance must activate in our recipe to prosper. Paul was so determined to finish his course that he wouldn't stay dead. I don't know what challenge you are facing today, on your road to success and prosperity, but I don't think you've been stoned.....to death. You may have gotten stoned or hung-over but probably not stoned to death. The point is it takes perseverance to finish our course,
it takes perseverance to prosper. Many times the winner is just the last man standing. The winner is the business that made it through the recession. The winner is the preacher who kept his zipper up while others fell. The winner is the athlete whose conditioning sustained his vigor in overtime.

Opportunities become realities only to people who refuse to give up even when they are facing overwhelming odds! Who like Paul will refuse to stay dead! Winston Churchill said, the nose of a bulldog is slanted backward so he can continue to breathe without letting go. When a bulldog latches onto something, he refuses to let go until his goal has been reached. And his nose is designed to allow him to keep breathing without letting go.

No matter what you are involved with, or how difficult it may seem, the Holy Ghost will keep pumping heavenly air into your lungs so you won't have to give up till you have finished your course and reached your goal. If only you will hold on. When God says in Ephesians 6 "Having done all to stand", he means for you to keep on standing. So if you are going to prosper you are going to have to persevere at times.

In Luke 8: 5-8a Jesus tells about a sower who sowed the word in different types of soil. The sower sows the word. Very little attention is given to the sower, it doesn't say if he was a flashy eloquent evangelist, or a pudgy little farm-boy, the important thing is that he was sowing God's word. That's all I am is a sower. Many churches today teach modern psychology dressed up in Christian clothes. Some of it is good, useful, even biblical, but thank God there's a few sowers left who sow the Word of God !

The word is the change agent in the parable and carries within itself the power to multiply and produce a crop. The word is called the seed in the parable but the attention isn't really focused on the seed because we don't have to tell the seed, "I'm gonna plant you in the ground now grow will you." The seed knows how to do that, in fact the seed carries within it a DNA code that is programmed to produce after it's kind; the carrot seed produces a carrot, the pea seed produces a pea, and a kernel of corn produces a corn stalk. The word of God is a living miraculous thing, it knows how to do it's work. The word preached concerning salvation is alive, encoded and full of power to produce salvation. The word preached concerning healing will produce healing. The word preached concerning prosperity is alive, encoded, and full of power to produce prosperity.

Isaiah 55:10-11 As the rain and snow come down from heaven, and do not return to it without watering the earth making it bring forth and bud, that it may give seed to the

110

sower and bread to the eater: So shall my word be that goeth forth out of my mouth; it shall not return unto me void, but it **shall accomplish** that which I please, and **it shall prosper** in the thing for which I sent it.

The word sent will **accomplish something !**
   The word sown will **prosper and produce a harvest !**

The word is the power and the change agent in the parable but the attention isn't focused on the word because there is never a problem with the word, it's good seed that will produce. The attention in the parable is focused on **the care of the ground.** Proper care of the ground is the difference between a bumper crop, a marginal crop, or complete crop failure.

I have a friend whose garden is the envy of the valley. His garden overflows with delectable harvest. Tasting how good it was, I decided to take up gardening and even talked him into giving me some of his carefully cultured seed. In my garden however, which was full of crab grass and cabbage worms, the same seed did not produce well. Same seed, different harvest due to the care of the ground.

Producing a harvest from God's word has to do with keeping the crab grass and cabbage worms from taking over your heart. (Ground Care) It also has to do with perseverance.

In explaining his parable in verse 11-15 Jesus said each ground encountered a time of testing. The ground which produced the harvest heard the word, retained the word, and by persevering produced a harvest; 30,60, or 100 times what was sown.

The primary difference between the hundredfold harvest and the terminated harvest lay in the fact that the good ground persevered.

Each ground did great for awhile,
   each harvest started off well.
      But when adversity, obstacles, distractions,
         persecutions, or a time of testing came,
            the non persevering soil remained sidetracked,
             remained distracted, remained defeated.

Even the good and noble heart receives adversity and persecution.

Even the good and noble heart gets attacked by that seed stealing devil.

Even the good and noble heart gets sidetracked into sins' deception at times.

But the good and noble heart says,
   when I fall I shall arise,
      when I get distracted I'll get refocused,
         when the word in my heart get's snuffed out,
            I'll go to church or my Bible and get more word.
              When persecution comes, it will not stop me.
              When the going gets tough, I'll get tougher.
              When a time of testing comes
              I'll persevere.
              Though obstacles arise,
              I will overcome them !

So my friends what makes all the difference is this quality called perseverance !

"Tough times don't last but tough people do !" (Robert Schuller) Reporter to Jerry Rice, "what is your life's motto?" "Never quit" Jerry replied. He worked out *every* day.

The word quit is not in the vocabulary of winners. I heard a preacher say that the word quit is not even in the bible.   I checked for myself and found in Strong's Concordance the word quit does appear 6 times but never in the context of giving up.   In fact half of the references were like 1 Corinthians 16:13; watch ye, stand fast in the faith, **quit you like men, be strong**. The word literally means act manly. The NIV translates it *be men of courage.*   So even the word quit in the Bible means act manly !

I enjoyed reading Brett Farve's story.   Perseverance was such a big player in this champion's life. As Brett entered the college draft only small schools would have anything to do with him till 3 days before the deadline when Southern Miss took a chance on him as their seventh string quarterback. By game day he was third string, but when the starters stumbled he got his chance trailing Tulane 17-3. As a seventeen year old freshman he led them to victory. For several years he was the starter leading them to upsets even over perennial power Florida State. At the peak of his season, to avoid an oncoming car, he swerved, his car flipped and hit a pine tree. They broke the window and wrestled Brett's mangled body from the car. In the ambulance he asked if he'd ever play football again, many wondered, but he eventually recovered from the concussion, cuts, and cracked bone only to find he started getting sick after eating. Upon examination they found that part of his intestine had died and it had to be removed. He lost 34 pounds in six weeks yet two months after the accident he stepped in as Q.B. to face the crimson tide of Alabama. He was still 30 pounds underweight but he led his underdog team to a big upset. Afterwards famous Alabama coach Gene Stallings said, "You can call it a miracle, or a legend, or whatever you want to, I just know on that day Brett Farve was larger than life."

It wasn't a miracle, and it wasn't a legend, it was what the Bible calls perseverance;
this quality separates winners from losers,
it separates champions from could have beens,
it separates 100 fold harvests from harvests that die on the vine,
and someday it will even separate the saved from the lost.
Because God's word in Hebrews 12:1 says, "Therefore since we are surrounded by such a great cloud of witnesses, let us throw off everything that hinders and the sin that so easily entangles and run with perseverance the race marked out for us. Let us fix our eyes on Jesus, the author and perfecter of our faith, who for the joy set before him endured the cross. Consider him who endured such opposition from sinful men, so that you will not grow weary and lose heart.

We must not only begin this heaven bound journey. We must throw off everything that hinders, and the sin that so easily entangles, and run with perseverance the race marked out for us. In other words we must finish our course.

Here's a list of excuses that will keep you out of God' best for your life;
1. It's impossible.
2. It can't be done.
3. I don't have what it takes.
4. It's too risky.
5. What if it doesn't work ?
6. What if I lose everything I have ? (Seizing God Given Opportunities, Jerry Savelle - other nuggets from this ch. also from Jerry)

This last question was nicely answered by a pastor I know in Brooks, Alberta. Bill was a farm boy who sold tractors. After receiving Christ he felt led to leave the tractor dealership and begin a church. His church was received with unusual hostil-

114

ity by the townspeople. In the beginning he noticed many waved at him with only one finger. The church began to grow and Bill built a lovely new sanctuary. The townspeople burned it down. Bill lost all he had, now he had no job selling tractors, and no sanctuary to preach in. Pastor Bill and his congregation rebuilt it only bigger! I've been in his lovely 300 seat sanctuary with flourishing congregation, in a town of only 1200 people ! Pastor Bill persevered.

In 1870 Aaron Montgomery Ward was a dry goods salesman who worked in rural areas in the Midwest where rural people were often overcharged by local merchants who had a monopoly. He believed he could offer the same goods through the mail and be more competitive, so he put everything he had into stocking up on items and printing mailers which he planned to send to a fraternal group of farmers. As he was about to launch his new business the devastating Chicago fire of 1871 destroyed his stock and price sheets. Many would have stopped at that point but Ward convinced two sales associates to join him in the venture and reprinted his sheets and repurchased his supplies. In 1872 Montgomery Ward opened for business and by the turn of the century Montgomery Ward's 500 page "wish-book" was being mailed to a million homes with sales in the millions.

God exalts persistence. Heaven rewards perseverance. Just because prosperity or success is delayed in your life does not mean it is denied. Just because your goal or dream does not come instantly is no sign it will never come. You have need of perseverance. Jesus said no man putting his hand to the plow and looking back is fit for service in the kingdom of God. God doesn't want you looking back he wants you going forward. Paul said one thing I do, forgetting things that are behind and pressing on into things that are ahead. I press on toward the goal to win the prize.

Spurgeon said, "through perseverance even the snail made it to the ark."

I pioneered a church in our local town. After 18 months my overseers talked me into giving it over to a more experienced pastor saying I would be the assistant pastor. After I gave it over there was no more talk of me being the assistant. That's OK I thought, I don't like being a pastor anyway. But then I started getting reports of my former flock; People I had led to Christ or was caring for backslid; one of them committed a murder. Another got drunk and was killed in a head on collision. This made me think I really was making a difference so I restarted another church from nothing and nobody. We got a pretty good congregation built up then at about the two year mark we had a church split that left us almost nothing.

The schism was so devastating to my wife that she broke out in a rash from head to toe. I had to send her to Korea to recover. At that time I wanted to quit, but I read a verse in a modern translation Bible that said, ***God comes to the aid of those who refuse to give up.*** I kept going and that Sunday a dear man got saved/recommitted who is still with us as a pillar and a deacon. We got built up good again then, when I went to do a large crusade to help two churches in Africa, we had another church split that left us with very little. It's no fun having a church of 40 drop to 9 but that one wasn't as hard to overcome since I'd done it before, but it was painful nevertheless. In some respects I've started over about 3 times but "God has come to the aid of those who refuse to quit." And today I can show you people who used to be on Meth, former alcoholics, and former disillusioned preachers who are now serving God as useful members of his eternal church because I didn't quit. (In retrospect part of the church splits were my fault as I was not discipling my key leaders every week like I am now.....even leaders will drift if we don't keep them on track and when leaders drift it can split a church. But I failed forward... I learned)

Your faith in God's word will cause you to outlast the devil. It's important to outlast the Devil because he's out to weary you and I, he's out to discourage. He wants you to turn chicken and quit. He wants you to wear out before he does. In some respects **the winner will be the last man standing.** One of the "glory days" kind of stories in my Willows family concerned my Grandpa, a tough rancher they called "Buckskin Jimmy Willows". A man named Bob Fittsimmons was a heavyweight fighter who later fought James Corbett in Nevada for the World Heavyweight Title. Before that fight Bob was barnstorming through Lewiston, Idaho. He offered $500.00 to anyone who could stay in the ring with him for 3 rounds.

In that era a "round" was not three minutes it was when one fighter knocked the other down. So getting knocked down and staying down was the only way to lose. That's the same way it is with us, **the only real way for us to lose is to get knocked down and stay down !** My grandpa "Buckskin Jimmy" not only survived the beating but got in a few good licks of his own. As Fittsimmons was handing him the $500.00 he told him, "Willows you should hang up that ranching and join me barnstorming you'd probably make a lot more money!" Micah 7:8 says *though I fall I shall arise,* and that attitude will help you outlast the devil and win in life. Perseverance in key if you want to *prosper in challenging times.*

As I contemplated what the E in this PROSPER acrostic was
going to stand for I thought E should stand for exercise. With
two thirds of Americans overweight, exercise would surely
help people prosper and be in health. I had a great quote
from authorities on the subject such as Jesse Duplantis.
Somebody told him, "there's no hope for my physique brother
Jesse, I think chubby is just in my genes." Jesse replied,
"looks like it's out of your jeans on this side over here !"
Jesse went on to say, "if you want to gain 5 pounds just go on
a diet. Just the sound of it makes you want to eat, **die......**et.
If you want to gain 10 pounds just go on a fast. Just think
about going on a fast and you'll gain weight !"

I also had a good quote from one of America's premier heart
doctors. He said, "the Bible says bodily exercise profiteth little, but that little is a lot when you consider the positive effect
it has on your heart.   20 minutes of aerobic exercise 3 times
a week will prolong your life and could save it."

So I thought exercise would be a good "E" candidate, because
you're sure not going to prosper in the earth if your dead.
But then I realized, if I preached on exercise I might lose
some of the tithers.

So I thought Enthusiasm.... Michael Jordan; life is a sport,
drink it up !   That's partly how I built a great business. Isn't
it funny how the world appreciates people of great enthusiasm
until it gets channeled into Jesus and the Church?   Then immediately it becomes suspect.   When you bring energy, zeal
and abandon to the Lord Jesus Christ you are thought to be a
fanatic. But in heavens' analysis who are the real mad ones ?

Is it not the complacent and self centered?   Enthusiasm...
sounds like love the Lord your God with all your heart, all
your mind, and all your strength.   The word enthusiasm
means God in you. People going after life with zeal as if God
were in them will I believe prosper.   But as much as I'd like
to speak on enthusiasm I knew there was an E word that was
even more pertinent to our prosperity, and the word is.....
drum roll...... Excellence.

Excellence; The quality of being outstanding.   Websters;
First Class, best of it's kind.
      synonyms;   exceptional, superior, above par, grade A.
Oral Roberts says, "the true work of God rolls forward on the
wheels of Excellence."

If you hold to a commitment to excellence in any field you
will prosper. The Hebrew word for excellence reflects nobil-
ity or worthiness. The classic Old Testament man of excellence was Daniel. Read Daniel 6:1-4 KJV; It pleased Darius
to set over the kingdom 120 princes, which should be over the
whole kingdom; And over these 3 presidents; of whom Daniel
was first; that the princes might give accounts unto them, and
the king should have no damage.
      Then this Daniel was preferred above the presidents and
princes, **because an excellent spirit was in him**: and the
King thought to set him over the whole realm.   Then the
presidents and princes sought to find grounds for charges
against Daniel in his conduct of government affairs, but they
were unable to do so. They could find no corruption in him,
because he was trustworthy and neither corrupt nor negligent.
Even his political rivals just could not dig up any dirt on Daniel because there wasn't any dirt to dig up ! He possessed an
excellent spirit with no occasion for accusation because he
was faithful and trustworthy. Negligence could not be found.

119

Daniel was a unique man in that most every other Old Testament hero had some kind of downfall; David fell with Bathsheba, Abraham told half truths concerning his wife, Moses lost his temper. But you cannot find any compromise or downfall in Daniel. At least not one that the scripture records.

I think all of us value the forgiveness offered in the New Covenant, I know I certainly do, but isn't it refreshing to find someone who doesn't just have a "Christian's aren't perfect just forgiven" bumper sticker, but they are actually living their life as an example of excellence. Daniel was just that kind of mentor.

The narrator sums up his life in Chapter 6:3 when it was declared of Daniel; "an excellent spirit was in him." An excellent spirit. People knew Daniel as a man with an excellent spirit. At one point in chapter 5 the king is terribly shaken because no-one can interpret his dream but the queen walks in and says, *cheer up, because during your fathers' reign there was a guy named Daniel in whom is an excellent spirit. He can interpret your dream.*

He had to be some kind of excellent to be remembered as excellent by a queen who had only heard of him from a previous administration. An extraordinary spirit the NAS. says.

Proverbs says guard your heart (spirit) with all diligence for out of it flow the issues (borders) of your life. As you and I place safeguards on our spirit where evil is concerned and begin to demand a high standard of our own life and conduct that excellent spirit will begin to establish a stronghold in our life and when it can be said of you that you have an excellent spirit - the prosperity will take care of itself. **This type of excellence will promote you and prosper your ways**.

All kinds of blessing, reward, honor, and position were accorded Daniel but it was really all just a byproduct of an excellent spirit and a commitment to excellence.

When you and I begin to aim for excellence in our spirit and begin to display excellence in our vocations we will inevitably prosper in all that we do.

Ya but pastor, there is a recession going on. Show me a man in whom is an excellent spirit and I'll show you a man who is prospering right in the middle of the recession.

Prov. 28:20 A faithful man will abound with blessings, but one eager for money will not go unpunished.   A big part of Daniel's excellence is that he was faithful, he was not negligent, and consequently he abounded with blessing. Begin to practice faithfulness in the little things; begin to get to work on time, to appointments on time, to church on time. Do you think God is less worthy than your employer? Follow through with commitments that you have made. Perform every task you are assigned in such a way that if your enemies were looking to dig up dirt on you they'd have to say, "dang there's not much dirt there, they're prompt, they're diligent, they're not negligent. We're just going to have to **make up something** to slander them with."

Do it right, because it's right, and then do it right.   Because when are you ever going to have the time to undo it and do it again?   In 2008 I was building our new 5,400 square foot showroom for HuckleberryLand -- at that time I gave this testimony; I'm trying right now to build a new business in time for the tourists. This urgency makes it very tempting to cut corners. Last week I wanted to pour the huge concrete slab but there was probably frost in the ground that would make the slab crack. I was tempted to just plunge forward and live with the results but as I was seeking God for wisdom, in our Wednesday evening meeting, Kenneth Copeland said, "do it right, because it's right, and then do it right. Because when are ever going to have the time to undo it and do it again?" That was a word from God to me because if you get concrete wrong, if you get the foundation wrong, then you will have problems that will NEVER go away. So I rented $500.00 worth of concrete tarps to defrost the ground for four days because I was aiming for excellence. I knew it was I who would have to live with the results.

Take the time to do things right in your life especially in the area of relationships. That is an area where if you get the foundation wrong you'll be dealing with problems the rest of your life. I've heard all the justifications for ignoring God's counsel, *Well it's been a long time since I was with a man,* I know we're not married but we love each other, the person became a christian because of us livin' together. Cutting corners is only going to hurt you in the long run. Quick and easy might be convenient for now but you'll be sorry later. So do it right, because it's right and then do it right because when are you ever going to have the time to undo it and do it again.

I've done a lot of things wrong in my life but one thing I did right. Before salvation I was a girl crazy sinner. But when I gave my life to Jesus I quit messing with girls and decided to keep myself pure till I met the godly, right girl. For seven long years I lived as a celebate, then when I did meet Jaekyung, we dated with honor and respect for over a year till the day we got married. While dating we had a list of very detailed rules that governed what we could and could not touch, and what we could and could not do! Taking the time and effort to do that one thing right has brought blessing after blessing into my life, and it will to your life also - if you take the time to get the foundation right for marriage.

Proverbs says a man's own folly ruins his life yet in his heart he rages against the Lord. Some people go down the wrong track like a runaway freight train and then when life explodes in their face they get mad at God.

Proverbs 1 says if you ignore Wisdom's counsel and reproof then wisdom will laugh at you when your calamity comes like a whirlwind. You'll be mad at God for a broken life and he'll say, "It was you dummy that ignored wisdom, don't get mad at me."

Well I'm only 16, you can't expect me to do things right can you ? Daniel was only a teen too yet he made a resolve to be the kid on campus who was sold out for God! Even in the the Babylonian University fast lane he resolved not to defile himself with the fare of the world. There are some sold out young people for God in this generation too. I heard a story from a reliable source of a guy in college livin' in a fraternity house and he was so sold out for God that he decided to go on a Daniel fast; where certain choice foods were no longer a part of his menu. An evening came where there were succulent eats being served at the house. He told God, "I'd like to go off this Daniel fast and chow down on some of this food, but if you'd like me to stay on it, show me and I will." He went across the hall to study in a quieter section and met a young man whose name was *"Daniel Fast!"* He took that as his confirmation to stay on the fast, which he did for another 2 years - till he saw God bring about significant changes on campus.

The spirit of Daniel - that excellence spirit - is coming on young people today who will dedicate themselves to a higher standard. In 2001 we had the privilege of meeting Shaun Alexander, the 2005 NFL MVP of the Seattle Seahawks.

He told the youth gathering that after coming off a record high school season, with 3500 yards rushing and 54 touchdowns, he was well known and the girls on the campus of the University of Alabama were crowding around him wanting some attention. But in the midst of temptation galore he said, "I kept walking the narrow path and to me it wasn't a hard choice because I know Satan's way is death no matter how good it looks and God's way is life and the fulfillment of my desires."

He kept himself holy in college and once in Seattle met the girl he felt was God's choice for his wife. In his book he tells this interesting account of their dating. By August, Val and I had been friends for two months. After having been to Seahawks training camp preparing for a preseason game, I came home on a Tuesday. That night something happened to me - something many people will think is totally bizarre - but it's true. I had a dream that night, and for the following two nights as well. In the dream that first night, I was sitting on the leather couch in my TV room. Valerie walked in and slid down over the arm of the couch next to me.
"Hey" she said.

We looked at each other. Then I pulled her close, and we started to kiss. Soon we went to the bedroom and had sex. When we were finished , I got up and walked over to the mirror, angry at myself. In the dream I stared at myself , thinking, I'm a Christian. What am I doing? How could I let this happen?

The next night I had the same dream with the same results. Afterward I looked in the mirror angry at myself again. As I stared at my reflection, I heard the words, *if you hadn't kissed her, it never would have happened.*

On the third night I had the dream and heard the words again.

On Sunday she dropped by. When she walked in, I was sitting on the black leather couch in my TV room. I hadn't even been thinking about the dreams. Then she slid down the arm of the couch - and the three dreams flooded back into my mind. I was totally shaken. It's happening. The dream is coming true. Now what ?

She took a deep breath gazed right at me and said, Shaun, God told me we shouldn't kiss each other until we're married."

My mouth dropped open. I was unable to say anything for a second. Then I shook my head. "Valerie, you won't believe this , but.... And then I told her about the three nights of dreams.

The understanding we reached that night became the basis for our dating life and we didn't kiss till the marriage ceremony. (Touchdown Alexander, Harvest House Publishers, Page 139 - 141)

Later he tells how he flew her to New York City and proposed to her in a horse and carriage riding through central Park. The Devil and the world want us to think that instant gratification is the big prize but that actually bypasses some of the tension, the romance, the curious glances,... the things that really make a courtship memorable for a lifetime.

Shaun's testimony of not even kissing till the wedding day might seem extreme to some. We did plenty of kissing before the wedding so it's different than the rules which kept us holy, but I think Shaun's story reflects Romans 16:19; Be excellent at what is good, be innocent of evil and the God of peace will soon crush satan underneath your feet. The Greek word excellent there means surpassing or more than.   Our kids have sometimes complained, "your standards for movies and family life are higher and more strict than those of even our good

125

Christian friends." Good that's one of the definitions of the word excellence, "more than." Shaun's guidelines with his bride may have been MORE THAN the average, even for believers, but that's the stuff NFL MVP's are made of. Our son, Josiah, just got accepted to Williams College. Williams has an 18% acceptance ratio and is tied with Amherst as the #1 liberal arts college in the nation. Our "more than" commitment as a family has paid off.

1. Excellence involves dedication... Do it right, because it's right, then do it right.

Foundation....God's solid foundation stands firm, sealed with this inscription; "The Lord knows those who are his," and, "Everyone who confesses the name of the Lord must turn away from wickedness." In a large house there are vessels not only of gold and silver, but also of wood and clay; some are for honorable purposes and some for dishonorable purposes. If a man cleanses himself from unclean and contaminating influences he will be a vessel of honor, made holy, useful to the master, and prepared for every good work. 2 Timothy 2:19-22

In a great house, such as God's church, there are vessels of honor, such as gold goblets used for fine dinners, and there used to be clay bedpans used for urination. Some for noble purposes, others for urinating in.

Some say, "not everybody can be a vessel of honor, maybe I'm just a little clay pot for Jesus." No, the truth is you and I determine what kind of vessel we will be. Verse 21 says if we purge OURSELF of dishonorable, degrading activity such as youthful lusts THEN we can have the privilege of being a vessel of honor. Consequently as Christ's representatives we must become ready, willing, and dedicated to expecting and

126

demanding the highest form of excellence of ourselves. So excellence involves dedication. Mediocre happens without trying but excellence requires dedication.

You will not find a person of excellence late on paying bills or asking for a preacher's discount. A person of excellence will pay whatever price it takes to represent the Lord Jesus well as a vessel of honor.

#2 Excellence involves honor,

Honor involves what you and I will do in a tight spot. When ethical compromise seems in our best interest what will we do. One of the big reasons Daniel had an excellent spirit is he wouldn't compromise his values even when it was going to land him in the Lion's den or the fiery furnace. Sometimes I'm tempted to not tell the whole truth just to avoid correction from my wife, but Daniel wouldn't compromise even if he had to face the fiery furnace.

God's word says the integrity of the upright guides him. You don't have to pray about most decisions. There should be a set of values in your life that makes up something called integrity, which then guides and directs your decisions.

Excellence involves honor. Kenneth Copeland tells of a time when another individual in the insurance company his father worked for began to flatter and lure his father away from the present company, and offered him stock worth millions of dollars if he'd branch out with him.

The company had strict policy against this and sued the usurper. A.W. Copeland was the deciding witness. If his testimony incriminated the accused A.W. would lose millions. Young Kenneth said, "I wondered what Dad would do, I knew millions of dollars were at stake, I watched as my Dad took the stand. He wasn't a bit nervous or anxious. He didn't have any sweat breaking out on his brow. I couldn't believe he could be so calm."

The lawyer asked the question: "Did this man offer you a job with his new company doing the same thing that you are doing now?" Without a second's hesitation Dad answered "yes, he did." When it was over, he stood up and walked away. He left all that money lying on the table and the stock untouched. Amazed Ken asked him, Dad, how did you keep from saying what that man wanted you to say?" He replied simply,

"It would have been a lie." It was as simple as that. To get the money, the stock, the position, Dad would have had to lie. There was never any question in his mind. He went right on with his humble sales position. He gave no more thought on the matter. Every time he would see the man he testified against, he would walk up, shake his hand and ask how the new company was coming along. That man had such a respect for my dad: he loved my dad all his life. (Honor - Walking in Honesty, Truth and Integrity, Harrison House, Kenneth Copeland, p.23-24)

One more good example involving Shaun Alexander; Not long after I agreed to go to Alabama on a scholarship, a representative from Florida State phoned. "We know you verbally told Alabama you'll go there, but it's not signing day yet and we have a situation here that might interest you. We have signed the best quarterback, Dan Kendra, and the best wide receiver, Randy Moss. Both of them had verbal agreements before checking us out but changed once they saw the potential here. With you as running back we'd have the best in all three positions, does that interest you ?" Shaun replied, "although I really appreciate the offer," I said, interrupting his pitch, "I've given Alabama my word." My mother's teaching and the lesssons I'd learned in church were so strong, I didn't even feel tempted. To give my word is as strong as signing a contract. (Ibid., page 52-53) Incidentally Alabama with Alexander beat the Gators 40-39 breaking the Gators' 30 game win streak and their six-year streak of home wins.

What will you and I do in a tight spot? When something we want, or a lot of money is at stake? Excellence involves honor and integrity.

In high school we had a course for one whole semester called situation ethics. For 45 minutes per day a pale faced agnostic teacher, with long red hair, would ask the class to make moral decisions after he'd present us with various fictitious situations. As a class we'd evaluate the pros and cons then come up with what seemed to be the most beneficial choice - often it was the path that seemed to create the least friction and benefit the most people. The 10 commandments were never consulted - right and wrong were determined by majority vote. A couple months later I became a Christian and started reading the Bible for the first time in my life. I found there that right and wrong are not determined by majority vote.
Right and wrong are not determined by which option makes the least waves.
Right and wrong are not determined by which option is the most profitable.
Right and wrong are determined by the word of God which says;

THOU SHALT NOT LIE.

THOU SHALT NOT STEAL.

THOU SHALT NOT BEAR FALSE WITNESS.

THOU SHALT NOT COMMIT ADULTERY.

Our nation is awash in situation ethics. But in this day and hour, God needs some voices crying in the wilderness of

129

moral relativity. God is wanting the church of Jesus Christ to rise up; not as high profile con men, or tongue talkers who deal dirty, but as vessels of honor, vessels of excellence and vessels of integrity.

If we are to be people of excellence we must become people of honor and integrity. I once faced a terrible test in our business. I was buying pickup loads of Huckleberries from a guy in Idaho. The picker claimed one load was two days old but after a couple days in the fridge I looked at them and they were moldy. Huckleberries were $20.00 a gallon at the time so you can imagine what a pickup load was worth. The temptation was to can them up quick and keep my mouth shut. Instead I called the owner of the *"drive in with the bears"* park and asked, How would your bears like a whole bunch of wild Huckleberries ? I lost hundreds of dollars but when it was over I still had my integrity and the bears were very happy.
A decision like that may seem opposite to "prospering" but I think in the long run a commitment to excellence as a company pays off.

This all has to do with a solid foundation just like my concrete foundation story. GOD WANTS A FOUNDATION in our lives that he can afford to build upon. But if our foundation is CROOKED God can not afford to build much on it.
God wants to build something of strength and longevity in your life but he needs a foundation of honor and excellence.

This is a convicting message. I myself got convicted on certain points. If you did too let's remember Jesus dealing with the lady caught in adultery. Sometimes you and I get caught up in things that we know are second class but our flesh just seems to overpower our better judgement. If you find yourself snared in mediocre morals Jesus says to you, "neither do

I condemn you." But he also says, "go and sin no more." (Though he forgives our sin some sin requires restitution. Before I was a Christian I was a compulsive shoplifter. When I gave my life to Christ I sold my sports car and repaid many establishments.)

3. Excellence will do what it takes to be well above average.

Excellence means above average. John Maxwell was inspired by a quote from English Prime Minister Benjamin Disraeli, "To be conscious that you are ignorant of the facts is a great step to knowledge." John realized his need to grow in the field of leadership. In 1969 he wrote the top ten leaders in his field and offered to pay them $100.00 each for a half hour of their time so that he could ask them questions. For the next several years he and his wife Margaret planned every vacation around where these people lived. If a great leader in Cleveland said yes to his request they'd vacation in Cleveland. This above average commitment to glean truth in his field has led to Maxwell being a highly sought after speaker and writer. (The 21 Irrefutable Laws of Leadership, John Maxwell, page 25)

The average leader might buy and read a book. To spend several years of vacations paying leaders money to interview them is above average. Excellence will do what it takes to be well above average.

1. Excellence involves dedication... Do it right, because it's right, then do it right.

2. Excellence involves honor.

3. Excellence will do what it takes to be well above average.

ℜ.eap   Chapter 12

The word reap means to harvest a crop.

Are you harvesting a crop? Are you a harvester? You can be. The word also means TO RECEIVE, TO OBTAIN, TO REALIZE.

Hebrews 10 says we are not among those who draw back but we are among those who THROUGH FAITH AND PATIENCE RECEIVE and inherit the promises. So we're not drawing back but we are obtaining what's been promised, we are receiving a harvest in the earth.

Psalm 126 paints a beautiful picture about reaping;

When the Lord brought back the captives to Zion, we were like men who dreamed. Our mouths were filled with laughter, our tongues with songs of joy.

Then it was said among the nations, "The Lord has done great things for them." The Lord has done great things for us and we are filled with joy.

He who goes out weeping, carrying seed to sow,

Will return with songs of joy, carrying sheaves with him.

That my friends is what reaping is all about; joy, laughter, friends, and neighbors saying, "wow, look what the Lord has done for them!" Fortunes which you may have previously sowed into the kingdom are now being restored and coming back to you on waves of God's blessing and increase - you may have sown in tears but now you are reaping with shouts of joy !

Gal 6:9 says Let us not be weary in well doing, for in due season we shall **surely reap** if we faint not.

It doesn't say, maybe we'll reap if the economy is good that year, It doesn't say maybe we'll reap if people like us. No, it says in due season we shall surely reap if we faint not.
Say, "I shall *surely reap*! *If I faint not!*"

The word reap also means **to receive a reward or benefit as a consequence of one's own or other people's action.**

The Final R in this acrostic message on the word PROSPER is for REAP. Because REAPING is the reward you receive if you put the earlier steps of this series into action;
All the **P**. lanning.
All the **R**. idding yourself of a poverty mentality.
All the seizing of **O**.pportunity.
All the order and **O**. rganization.
All the **S**. owing.
All the **P**.erserverance.
All the **E**.xcellence, uprightness, and honor.
put you in a position to **R**EAP a mighty harvest on the earth !

Hebrews 10:35, Cast not away your confidence, which hath **great recompense of reward.** You need to persevere so that when you have done the will of God you will receive what he has promised.
When you've done the P, the R, the O, the S, the E, then just add the Perseverance - and you will surely get to the last R which is the time of REAPING.

Do not therefore fling away your fearless confidence for it carries with it a great and glorious compensation of reward, a great PAYDAY. We have employees who work for us on an hourly basis. Some of them have to send their time card in every Tuesday to "Express Personnel Services." They are the paymaster - and the paymaster knows how many hours they've worked. The Employee also knows how many hours they've worked, and they expect to receive what the time card indicates. The books are kept accurately and properly and they are paid according to what they are entitled to.

Jeremiah 51:56 says; For the Lord is a God of recompense, He will fully repay.
He is keeping the books and will fully repay. He will reward every act of faith you have been involved in. He's watched every time you have been under Satanic pressure in the middle of the night yet you have continued to go forward !
God watched that.
God saw when you were thinking, man I need to spend my tithe on gas, I need to buy the kids some clothes, but I'm not going to do it because my Bible says I need to tithe - and I'm not going to be a robber of God. What you did by faith and sometimes under great pressure God watched, God marked your time card, and payday is a coming !

In other words if you do what the Word teaches and you stayed faithful in it then you can expect a payday!

Your labor in the LORD is not in vain. 1 Corinthians 15:58

Here's a few examples of REAPING in the Bible;

* So Joshua took the entire land, just as the Lord has directed Moses.
* The Lord gave them rest on every side, just as he had sworn to their forefathers.
* NOT ONE of their enemies withstood them
* The Lord handed all their enemies over to them

* Then the land had rest from war.   Joshua 21:44 and 11:23

* So David recovered everything the Amalekites had taken including his two wives. Nothing was missing: young or old, plunder or anything else that had been taken. He took all the Amelakite's flocks and herds and his men drove them ahead of other livestock saying, This is David's plunder. The Lord gave David victory wherever he went.   I Samuel 30:19-20

* The apostles performed many miraculous signs and wonders among the people. They were highly regarded by the people. More and more men and women believed in the Lord and were added to their number.   As a result, people brought the sick into the streets and laid them on mats so that at least Peter's shadow might fall on some of them as he passed by. Crowds gathered also from the towns around Jerusalem.

Acts 5:12-16

* After Job had prayed for his friends, the Lord made him prosperous again and gave him twice as much as he had before... The Lord blessed the latter part of Job's life more than the first.... Nowhere in all the land were there found women as beautiful as Job's daughters.   Job 42:10-11

* When the men of Judah came to the place that overlooks the desert and looked down toward the vast army they saw only dead bodies lying on the ground; no one had escaped. So Jehoshephat and his men went to carry off all their plunder, and they found among them a great amount of equipment and clothing and also articles of value - more than they could take away.   There was so much plunder that it took three days to collect it.   Then they assembled at the valley of Beracah (praise) 2 Chronicles 20:24-26 (This was the result of a corporate fast and praise and worship.)

* During the seven years of abundance in Egypt the land produced plentifully... Joseph stored up huge quantities of grain
like the sand of the sea; it was so much that he stopped keeping records because it was beyond measure. And Joseph had
two sons the first Manasseh; "God has caused me to forget my
trials" and the second, Ephraim; "God has made me fruitful in
the land of my suffering." Genesis 41:46-52 (This was the
reaping portion of just one God given plan.)

* The weight of the gold that Solomon received yearly was
25 tons, not including the revenues from the merchants and
traders and from all the Arabian kings and the governors of
the land. The people of Judah and Israel were as numerous as
the sand on the seashore; they ate, they drank and they were
happy. Solomon's daily provisions were 185 bushels of fine
flour and 375 bushels of meal, ten head of stall-fed cattle and
a hundred sheep and goats, as well as deer, gazelles, roebucks
and choice fowl. Judah and Israel lived in safety, each man
under his own vine and fig tree.
King Solomon was greater in riches and wisdom than all the
other kings of the earth. The whole world sought audience
with Solomon to hear the wisdom God had put in his heart.
Year after year, everyone who came brought a gift - articles of
silver and gold, robes, weapons and spices, and horses and
mules. The king had a fleet of trading ships at sea. Once
every three years it returned carrying gold, silver and ivory,
and apes and baboons. Segments from 1Kings

I could go on but I feel like the writer of Hebrews eleven;
time would fail me to tell of the widow's jar of oil that flowed
till she was debt free, of the siege that was lifted when four
lepers marched out in faith, of the Israelites plundering the
silver and gold of the Egyptians, of the miraculous catches of

fish....... of Gideon, Samson, and Barack who through faith subdued kingdoms, wrought righteousness, stopped the mouths of lions and obtained what was promised.

SO REAPING is about OBTAINING what is promised through faith! The Bible in your lap is full of amazing promises and I'm praying you will be a single minded believer who will be tenacious enough to possess your land of promises.

The exciting part about the definition of reaping is that it is to receive a reward or benefit as a consequence of *one's own* or ***other people's action.***

As believers we also obtain a benefit and reward as a consequence of OTHER PEOPLE's actions. You may not have lived life perfectly but JESUS DID, and by receiving him through faith YOU GET WHAT HE DESERVED!

You get heaven instead of hell,

You get your prayers answered,

You get favored son status,

You become a JOINT HEIR of all that JESUS the firstborn son is entitled to.

That's why they call the gospel good news!

You and I get what the perfect one deserved!

You and I reap the blessing of Jesus' actions.

As I bring this series to a conclusion, I don't want you to just go through the steps that will lead to your prosperity but then fail to close the deal and actually REAP!

Maybe you know someone, or maybe that someone is you, who is great at coming up with a business plan or prospectus but they never make any money. They're the guy who can dribble the length of the court just fine but they always miss the lay-up. They're the one who can land a good job but never keep the job. They can come to the brink of success again and again but never can quite close the deal. I don't want that person to be you.

For much of my life I've made my money as a carpenter. Nothing wrong with being a carpenter - good honest work - Jesus was a carpenter. In fact it's important that Jesus' vocation was a carpenter, like really how would you feel if your savior had been a tele-marketer ? The tele-marketer from Nazareth just claimed he's the light of the world !, It just doesn't fit. Or how would you feel if he'd been a CEO, an NBA star, a lawyer, an IRS auditor, a politician, a multi level marketer? Even if he'd been the guy who worked at McDonalds it just would not have fit - but Jesus the carpenter just sounds right.

While living in Anchorage, I decided I'd been a carpenter long enough! I decided to make a living with my mind and tongue instead of my hands. I became a salesman. Selling family photo album packages. I quickly found out that what separated the men from the boys in sales was being able to close the deal. The technique we were taught was that you'd get them saying YES as you made the presentation. Can you see how this would benefit your family? Yes. Can you see that this would save you money in the long run? Yes. But then at the end, you would never ask them if they wanted it. Since they had said yes a couple times already you just assumed they wanted it and smoothly asked, "now would you like to pay cash, put this on your credit card, or simply make payments for $12.95 per month." Have you ever had that done to you ? It's a technique for closing the deal.

Closing a deal is an art. I got out of that kind of sales because I didn't really believe in selling people non-essentials on

138

credit, but closing the deal remained an important lesson for me that I later used to get Jaekyung to marry me. I closed the deal! I used to have moderate success as an evangelist but then God gave me a powerful message about spiritual freedom which is not only a great message but has an anointed way to close the deal and every time I give this message, in a good harvest field, many people receive Christ. (Over 200 people the first night at my last crusade in the Philippines.) For several years this was the only message I had which had a great close so I'd have a big altar call the first night and comparatively little response the second night. But then I developed another powerful message that has a great close and in the Philippines 150 people responded the second night. Even Josiah my son has preached my second night message with good success partly because the message has a great close.

Some people live their life giving a great presentation but they just can't close the deal. They seem to exercise faith but never really seem to OBTAIN what the word promises. They can run around just fine on the gridiron or basketball court but rarely score any points. They sow seeds but never really reap the harvest. They're like a golfer who can make a great drive, get on the green in two shots, but then take five strokes to sink the putt. (Too many self sabotage because of a failure to implement step two; Rid yourself of a poverty mentality. If you think money is evil you will self sabotage before reaping. As for me I'm 100% convinced I can serve God better rich that I can broke.... when you get to that place you won't self-destruct.)

If you implement these steps it will change your status and revolutionize your world. So friends when it comes to prospering as your soul prospers I don't want you learning all the steps to get there but then fail to actually cross that threshold and REAP a harvest !   So I'm going to talk about three hindrances to reaping;

1. Not paying attention to or following God's Commands.

Deuteronomy chapters 28 - 29 speak about the blessings of following God's way and the curses associated with not conforming our lives to his will.

Deuteronomy was a binding covenant between God and Israel regarding God, the landlord's, terms which would govern his gift of the promised land to the nation of Israel.   But these blessings and curses also seem to work their way into our lives today. Take a moment and read Deuteronomy 28: 1-13

That my friends sounds like reaping;

v.2 Blessings overtaking you.

v. 3 Blessed in the city and blessed in the country - sounds like the person is involved in commerce or ministry that took him to both rural and urban areas.

v. 4 A blessing on your family and everything you do vocationally.

v. 6 Blessed when you come in and blessed when you go out. Those who are "planted in the house of God" will flourish according to Psalm 92 but for this verse to activate you need to take some trips. Two thirds of God's name is GO. And God blesses those who obey the great commission.   A couple came with me to Africa on a mission trip. They did not have any spending money but at our layover in Seattle the wife found a $50.00 bill on the floor of the airport restroom. She repeatedly asked people if it was theirs but after no-one claimed it she had spending money !   On another mission trip my son and I were to stay at a little bungalow in Kruger National Park in South Africa. The regular bungalows were all booked so they upgraded us to the presidential bungalow!

140

Mission trips are not the only time we believe for blessings. Even on ordinary business trips we claim we are blessed going out and coming in and that God makes us a blessing. On one such business trip we mentioned our son was fast, (Abe has never been beat in a 50 yard dash even in Atlanta.) Someone said they'd give him $20.00 if he could beat the fast kid in Pasco, Washington. Abe beat him and had an extra $20.00 ! We also like to be a blessing, in Spokane recently a haggard single mother was gassing up her beat up car. As she went in to pay I threw some bills through the open window onto the drivers seat.   As she was coming out I heard her kids merrily screaming, "Mom that man was throwing money in through the window !"

v. 8 The Lord will send a blessing on your garage and your savings account.   God promises to "command" a blessing on your savings account so why don't you start one.

v. 10 Abundant prosperity will be on your children and all you do.   Say "abundant prosperity."   The verse says the abundant prosperity will cause people around you to be kind of afraid of you.   God has done that for my wife because I'm kind of afraid of her at times! Ha Ha!

v. 12 The weather will cooperate in order to bless you. I've noticed the weather cooperating with my building projects.... I've also noticed the enemy using the weather to hinder me at times and I have to be tougher than his hindrance.

v. 12 All the work of your hands will be blessed. Look at your hands and see what amazing inventions of God they are. God promises to bless the work of your hands. Tell someone, "work is not a four letter word."

v. 12 You will lend to many but borrow from none. In my city five railroad employees each put in $5.00 and started lending money on interest to their buddies. Today what they started has several branches with assets of over one billion dollars. People in the church should start their own credit union and get rich just by lending to many but borrowing from none. "Churches in Covenant" I belong to is considering launching out in this capacity. covenantchurch.org

v. 13 The Lord will make you the head and not the tail but it's totally contingent on what comes next IF, say "IF," **IF you pay attention to the commands of the Lord your God that I give you this day and carefully follow them..** you will be *always on top never on bottom.* Are you tired of being on bottom rather than on top? If so make a quality decision to pay attention to and follow God's commands. Our country is currently exhausting it's options for reversing the depression, but **this option** is what made us great once and would do so again.

Conrad Hilton, the founder of the Hilton hotel chain, is a man whose life is governed by certain laws. One law is to never make a business decision after dinnertime. Another law is to go to his church and pray every morning and to be there for the services. He's paying careful attention to Gods' commands and God has made him the head and not the tail. But he's a Catholic? God will bless a Catholic who pays attention to and follows God's commands much more than he will bless a careless charismatic.

Now let's look at the curses in Deuteronomy 28:15-20 (Full list of curses goes through verse 68)

God says, "because you did not serve the Lord gladly in the time of prosperity now you will be cursed." Prosperity is a blessing but it's also a test. Israel failed the test and so has our nation in many respects. But they later repented and were restored and the U.S.A. can too.

142

The curses are in many cases the exact reciprocal and reverse of the blessings. They sound like Newton's law, if anything can go wrong it will. Verse 29 says *you will be unsuccessful at everything you do.* Do you know anyone like that ? Unsuccessful in all they do. That summarizes the curse.

What does verse 30 represent ? Pledged to be married but another will ravish her. Pledged to be married - you went through all the steps - found a guy or girl you liked, spent money on courting them, bought a ring and set a date, but before you REAP the joy of marriage it falls apart. You will build a house but will not live in it. It's hard and expensive building a house yet this person will fail to reap the benefit of all their hard work.

You will plant a vineyard but will not even begin to enjoy it's fruit. In other words you will go through all the steps but never close the deal. When you are ignoring and disobeying God and his word you have no foundation for lasting success.

So Deuteronomy 28 speaks of one guy that is blessed in all he does and another who takes one step forward and three steps back. Same land, same opportunities, yet one is blessed in all they do and the other can't win for losin'. The amazing thing is that each person gets to choose which path they will follow.

I once picked up a Native American hitch-hiker. He looked like he'd been recently beat up and had a few teeth missing. "What happened?," I asked. He replied, "I was recently divorced and then badly beat up." "Sounds rough, I'm sorry," I replied. He said, "it's the best thing that ever happened to me." "Why?" I asked. "Because through it all I came to know Jesus Christ--- In the midst of the worst of these trials my late Christian grandfather appeared to me in a dream wearing his buckskins. He held out a cross which had my name on it, "Leroy." On his left he showed me a wasted landscape with broken beer bottles littering the scorched, barren terrain. On his right was a pristine valley filled with game and beautiful homes. He held out the cross then said, "now Leroy you must choose your destiny." Leroy chose God's way and was hitchhiking to Browning to tell the First Nations people there to choose God's way.

It's scorched earth or pristine valley, black or white, dark or light, blessing or curse, to sum it up God said through Moses, See, **I set before you life and prosperity, death and destruction. DT. 30:15 Choose you this day whom you will serve,** Joshua 24:15 Make your choice.

There are other areas that will hinder you from reaping that we will touch on but this is the biggee so I put it first in priority. If you are willing and obedient you will eat the best of the land but if you resist and rebel, you will be devoured by the sword. Isaiah 1:20. I worked hard to buy ten acres of beautiful treed land and I've told my three kids, You will all receive an inheritance from our other assets but THIS LAND is for the willing and obedient. If by the time you are 30 you have continued to be in church twice weekly, and serve the Lord, each of you will get 2 1/2 acres of this land. God rewards obedience and closes the purse at disobedience so why shouldn't I ? What would have happened if the father of the prodigal son kept wiring his son money even when he was in disobedience ?

"Without our contact with God we are nothing. With it we are, a little lower than the angels, crowned with glory and honor." Conrad Hilton

Now let's explore the second hindrance to reaping;

2. You are in the Wrong Field

If something comes naturally to you and you're good at it give your effort to that thing.   Emerson says, "each man has his own vocation. The talent is the call....He inclines to do something which is easy for him, and good when it is done."

Finding this particular talent or vocation is the first step in the art of successful living. Great frustration and the feeling of failure can be present if we follow someone else's footsteps rather than our own.   Don't worry if it takes a little time to find your own niche !   The great hotelier Conrad Hilton started out as a banker and politician. George Washington began as a surveyor.   St. Peter the rock was first a fisherman. This is no invitation to become a drifter, a professional malcontent.   But every man has a right, a duty I would say to search humbly and prayerfully for the place where he fits into the divine pattern.

Don't worry what you haven't got in the way of talent. Find out what you do have !

A very poor Greek once applied as a Janitor in a bank in Athens. "Can you write" demanded the head of employment. "Only my name," said the fellow. He didn't get the job so he borrowed money to travel to the USA where he became very successful. Years later he held a press conference in his Wall Street offices.   An enterprising reporter said, "you should write your memoirs." The gentleman smiled, "impossible, I can't write." The astounded reporter replied, "just think how much further you could have gone if you could write."   The Greek said, "no if I could write I'd be a janitor in a bank in Athens." (Be My Guest, Conrad Hilton, 1957 Prentice Hall Press.)

There is a basic work ethic and faithful spirit that will make you fairly successful in anything you try - and if you don't have it you won't succeed anywhere. But on the other hand, we all have strengths and we all have weaknesses and if we can find a niche which suits us we will REAP more readily. One time Abe and I were on our way to watch one of the kid's music nights at their high school. Abe said, "Josiah's going to play the sax tonight and he's only played the sax for two weeks I hope he doesn't blow it." I replied, "he won't blow it, he'll do good, anything to do with music he's just as good at as you are with anything to do with sports." He did fine. A good father can recognize the individual bent of his kids, so spend some time with your natural father and your good father in heaven and let them help you identify the most productive path for you to run on. There are also tests that help identify your most marketable strengths and your passion.

In the Osage Indian tradition each brave, when coming to maturity, fasted and prayed that Wahkontah, the great spirit, would give him signs or dreams to indicate his purpose in life. Such signs and dreams were then brought to "The Lodge of Mystery," where the "little old men" (who were neither little nor old, but named themselves so for humility) interpreted their meaning with the young brave. Whatever was concluded from that meeting (which included prayer) became the young brave's "medicine" for life. It would be said of a man "He has good medicine" or "His medicine is weak." (The Elijah Task, John and Paula Sandford, Logos International, page 181)

In the same way we can seek God for our purpose in life. I had a room-mate in Anchorage Alaska. He was brilliant and got a full ride to Ohio State (Buckeyes) then went on to a scholarship at medical school to become an M.D. In his second year of medical school he thought, I'm about to be a doctor and am still a virgin.... I should get some firsthand knowledge of sex. He did and soon became, in his words, "a pervert who couldn't think about anything else." He dropped out of school and ended up on the streets of Anchorage Alaska where Christians from the "Abbot Loop Christian Center" witnessed to him. He received Christ and rebuilt his life as part of this great church for several years. Though middle aged, he wanted God's best for his life so he fasted and prayed for a week. He was skinny to start with but looked like a refuge after a week of fasting ! God showed him to go to physicians assistant school which he did. After graduation he got a great job in Stow, Ohio and is very fulfilled. The gift is the call, even when the call was diminished by sin God restored the years the locust had eaten and brought him into a fruitful place.

3. Sabotage -- the third hindrance to reaping.

We all have a little gauge inside of our mind and spirit that is what people call a set point. It is like a thermometer in that when it gets too cold the heat kicks on and when it gets warm enough it shuts the unit down. If we begin to live below our mind set and expectation level we challenge ourself to rise up and be and do more. On the other hand if life starts to become bigger and better than we are accustomed to then we exceed the inner gauge and begin to undermine ourself until we sabotage and self-destruct back to the level that our thermometer is set. (Most of us self sabotage the same way nearly every time wether it's alcohol, porn, inferiority, or laziness - that's why it's important to know your own achilles heel and spend some time strengthening yourself in that department.) Various factors influence how our set point gets programmed including upbringing, what family and friends have spoken over us, expectations of teachers and mentors, past success or failure, and what spiritual teachers we allow to have input into our lives and ears. This is how a set point in "normally" programmed but the exciting truth is that you don't have to let other people and life's circumstances program your set point. You can take charge of your own destiny and program your set point to the level you desire then begin to live your life according to the set point you program - and not according to the set point life set for you.

In cultures like India the caste system has tried to socially and financially program people's set point, but America has been known as a land of opportunity where each man or woman can go as far, or be as much, as their own heart and spirit desire. Especially as adopted sons and daughters of the King of Kings we need not place limits on ourselves since God certainly does not. The teachers we listen to will greatly influence our set point. For this reason Jaekyung and I regularly travel to conferences which expose us to those who challenge our set point. (This subject is covered in detail under the Rid section of this teaching and by a book called, *Sabotage, that nasty little secret that is holding us back*--Mike Connaway)

REAP that harvest.
Choose the blessing - pay attention to and obey God's commands.
Locate the talent which is your call.
Develop that gift and talent.
Take control of your own set point.
Set it high, then don't self sabotage
when you START TO REAP!

Find a way to win even in the challenging times which face us today. Close the deal; you who have sowed in tears go forward and **reap** with shouts of joy. *"In everything David did he had success, because the Lord was with him."* 1 Samuel 18:14

Buddy the Outlaw   James, Jaekyung, Esther, Josiah, Abe

James grew up the son of an evolution preaching valedictorian who had become successful in business. When his mother had a stroke, parental supervision almost ceased and 12 year old James, nick-named "Buddy", slid into a routine of drugs, alcohol, and all night parties. After a drug related gang style fight, where he faced potential death at the wrong end of a 357 magnum, God began to reach out to "Buddy." James accepted Christ, was radically transformed, and has travelled to over 30 countries sharing in large crusades, in churches, on T.V., and in prisons, the true freedom that only Jesus can bring. While in Africa, he met and courted a lovely South Korean girl named Jaekyung Bae; daughter of well-known movie director, Sokin Bae. After a season of being very poor missionaries, James and Jaekyung started a little fruit stand in their carport called "HuckleberryLand" which has grown to become a large, successful, tourist superstore with a new

5400 square foot showroom (In Hungry Horse, Montana near Glacier Park). They also pioneered and now pastor Love and Faith Church in Kalispell, Montana. Their oldest son, Josiah, has been accepted into #1 ranked, "Williams College." Their daughter Esther is a fine pianist, likes to laugh, and is a friendly sophomore in highschool. His youngest son, Abe, is a speedster who is gaining some national recognition in football.
James Graduated from The University of the Nations; S.B.S.   **Golf 08**

Made in the USA
Monee, IL
18 May 2021

68308682R00085